INNER
SYMPHONY

Annemarie O'Connell

BALBOA.
PRESS

A DIVISION OF HAY HOUSE

Balboa Press books may be ordered through booksellers or by contacting:

Balboa Press
A Division of Hay House
1663 Liberty Drive
Bloomington, IN 47403
www.balboapress.com
1 (877) 407-4847

ISBN: 978-1-5043-9770-4 (sc)
ISBN: 978-1-5043-9771-1 (e)

Print information available on the last page.

Balboa Press rev. date: 06/14/2018

Contents

Introduction

You Create Your Own Reality! Those words were hard to digest when I heard them shortly after a Stage IVb Ovarian Cancer diagnosis involving major surgery and traditional chemotherapy treatment in 2014. How could I possibly create this horrible reality when I spend my time maintaining a positive mindset? I enjoy living in the moment, I make a conscious effort to be aware of other people's feelings and I always have good intentions when making decisions. So when a Naturopath doctor and a retired scientist, both friends of my brother, said I created the sickness, I was furious…but also inspired. What does that even mean I create my own reality? What I understood it to be early in my journey is that I have a choice and say in my well being. Not just a choice of which doctors or hospitals to go to, but an actual say in my outcome. It felt liberating and empowering to know that respected scientists were saying there were options available other than chemotherapy. Deep inside my being I knew treating cancer with traditional medicine was a bandaid and that I should focus on why it showed up in the first place. Unfortunately, I never explored that concept thinking, what do I know? Sadly, I came out of remission so quickly in August 2015, even after aggressively treating my physical body traditionally. At that moment, I knew I needed to explore alternative ways to treating a disease and decided to learn what those two brilliant minds were speaking of.

The first course of action was to see if anyone had accomplished this feat and what steps they took. To my surprise, there were many books available written by so many beautiful people telling their stories. One common approach they focused on was monitoring the alkalinity of the body. I first heard about the importance of a body's pH level and the impact it has on the physical body from Richard, my brother's scientist friend. He explained that our body is like a swimming pool and in order to function properly it should maintain a pH level of 7.2. A pH less than 7.2 causes the body to become acidic allowing it to become a breeding ground for bacteria and viruses. He also explained keeping the body at a high pH level, or too alkaline, can cause imbalances as well. A pH of 7.2 is ideal. It's the pH level we are born with and ironically the pH of the ocean.

Along with alkalizing their bodies, people explained that making drastic changes to their diet was another key component that helped them heal. With so much information and opinions about food and its effects on the body, I knew I needed guidance to help me sort it all out. A dear friend of mine suggested working with a nutritionist and recommended me to Kasia who consulted me. Through her thorough blood analysis, knowledge of the physical body and knowledge of treating disease, she offered me hope and a plan. She too spoke of the importance of alkalinity. Her vast knowledge of disease and the body was like no other. Treatment included becoming a vegan, which meant I could not eat anything who had a mother or father, just raw food. I also had to cut sugar, coffee, dairy, meat and anything processed out of my diet. Oh yeah and wine. Let's just say I start my day with a cup of coffee and enjoy a recreational glass of wine with dinner on the weekends. This was extremely difficult for me, but I would think to myself when I felt challenged, what's the alternative? There were also protocols I had to follow in addition to the diet change. The regimen required much discipline and was not easy to do while I was working full time, managing 3 kids in college and one in elementary school. The protocols started at 4am and were administered throughout the day until bed time. The idea was to stay ahead of the disease by treating my body with many supplements and modalities every 2 hours. The protocols included nebulizing iodine, rubbing DMSO, a natural extremely potent oil, on my body at different spots, ingesting 130 supplements throughout the day, drinking large amounts of Apple Cider Vinegar, magnesium chloride baths at night, infra red sauna in the morning, coffee enemas and baking soda protocols.

I am excited to say that in October, after just three months of using these protocols, I went back into remission. My doctors had no explanation how my scan went from the cancer spreading to my liver and lung in August to unremarkable in October. I have my beautiful friend Kasia to thank for that. Unfortunately, the remission only lasted a few short months and in December, I was on a plane to California seeking other options. You see, although these modalities which are brilliant counterparts to chemotherapy and building your body's immunity do have much success. The stress of following them while working full time and raising a family outweighed all the benefits of the regimen. This program worked, but I started thinking after 4 months, if this is the way I have to live what is the point? My quality of life was built around foods I really did not enjoy and involved using protocols that limited me to what I could do daily. Again I was treating the symptoms and not the 'why'. I kept thinking, there has to be another way.

My cancer came back in December of 2015 and my doctors said if I didn't do the chemotherapy I have been denying I could pass the point of no return and possibly lose my life. So in January 2016, I did one treatment and found myself extremely ill due to the debilitating effects that chemotherapy has on my body. I felt deflated because I knew that I did have a clean scan following my nutritionist's protocols but at the same time kept thinking, who wants to live like this? With all the knowledge I gained from the benefits of alternative medicine, I also became educated fully on the side effects of chemotherapy. I lost two friends to ovarian cancer because their bodies could not sustain the side effects of the treatments so to me, it was a losing decision no matter which path I choose. I knew that prolonged chemotherapy treatment takes its toll on a body and if I decided to continue my nutritionist's protocols, which were costly and expensive, I would be depriving myself of the life I wanted to live. Neither scenario was a win for me and I was losing hope fast.

A dear friend stopped by my house and saw the shape I was in. He strongly suggested I see someone, a friend/healer in Arizona who could help. He did not say much and I did not ask much. I am a woman of Faith and believe in miracles and decided literally in a moments notice that I would go visit her. I was scheduled to receive 8 more chemotherapy treatments every 2 weeks but just did the one and chose to go to Arizona instead. He sponsored the trip for me and next thing I knew I was on a plane to see a woman named Anita and about to embark on my Spiritual Awakening.

Even though I had a fever and could not function, I felt a sense of ease when I arrived on Anita's doorstep. There was something I felt in her house which brought peace throughout my body. I literally collapsed on her treatment table where she spent hours working on me. I spent 4 days in Arizona, and spent most of the day with her. I also participated in some detox therapy and lymphatic massages at local places. Most of the day Anita spent educating me. She introduced the work of Esther/Abraham Hicks, Joel Goldsmith, Wayne Dyer, Anita Moorjani, Dr. Bruce Lipton, Gregg Braden, Dr. Emoto and many other beautiful teachers. I left there 4 days later a new person. I was healed; my body transformed as if nothing ever happened. This was a miracle! I came home literally uplifted and glowing because I was taught material that opened my mind to many possibilities. The work she taught me is nothing new; it actually is as old as the beginning of time, it's just not in the mainstream….yet.

There are so many miraculous events that occurred leaving my family, friends and doctors in awe wondering how is she still alive? Through my experiences, I now know beyond a doubt that anyone can create a life they can only imagine it to be. I am not going to go into any more detail because the purpose of this book is to keep it short, and to the point. You see this workbook is something that I wish was available for me when I started my journey. Especially early on when I would spend my days walking around and wondering what should I be doing to help myself heal? For me, treating the physical body was like putting bandaids on symptoms and not a solution. I would often say that I wanted to understand why the disease presented in the first place but never understood how to do that until I met Anita. She taught me that disease is a body's way of saying pay attention, you have something you need to address, not on a physical level but on a cellular and emotional level. I have been asked many times to write something that people could follow on a daily basis and knew once it was time that I would write a short simple book to provide a roadmap. I continue trips to Sedona still today and am so grateful for my introduction to Anita and all the beautiful minds she exposed me to. This workbook is designed to be simple, short and to the point. It is a gift to you because you are the creator of your own reality. For me, it was about disease but it can be applied to any thing you are wanting to change or manifest into your life. Let's get started so you too can create your life as you want it to be. I wish you Many Blessings from the heart and know that you can be anything you want to be…...Just Believe it to be true….And So It is.

CHAPTER 1

Why this Workbook was Created

Where Do I Start?

After my encounter with an amazing spiritual teacher in Sedona who taught me that true healing comes from within, I focused my studies more on the mind and less on the body. I did have some success with doctors who treated my physical body, both traditionally and alternatively, but after discovering this new information I knew I needed to develop a deeper understanding of the body/mind/spiritual principles I was learning in Sedona. I attended multiple retreats over the past few years each time leaving more and more fascinated with the material I was exposed to. I would return home asking myself, "Why isn't anyone talking about these principles in my community?" Especially because so many lives were lost as a result of exhausting traditional options. As I continued my studies at home, I sifted through many books to find key ideas on how to achieve spiritual understanding and how it can affect our physical reality. I realized the teachers all spoke the same language and taught the same principals that have been around for many generations. Whether it was Ernest Homes' *The Science of the Mind*, John Randolph Prices' *Practical Spirituality* and *The Jesus Code*, Louise Hay's *Heal Your Body*, Jane Roberts' *Seth Speaks*, Dr. Wayne Dyer *The Power of Intentions*, Joel Goldsmith's *The Infinite Way*, or The *Law of Attraction* written by Esther and Jerry Hicks, they all offered the same beautiful message about the power of the mind and the Law of Attraction and how they alter one's physical reality. Understanding these principles not only play a necessary role in regards to healing but they also serve as a key tool to deliberately creating any reality you desire.

I was inspired to seek instructional clips on YouTube and found lectures from many of the great teachers I was introduced to in Sedona such as Abraham Hicks, Dr. Bruce Lipton, Dr. Masaru Emoto and Joel Goldsmith, to name a few. YouTube and my iPhone became a major tool in seeding my consciousness. I spent my days with earbuds in my ears listening to lectures becoming even more inspired and aware of the role we play in our own well being. This was a fantastic way to spend my day learning through audio and reading material, but unfortunately, I still was not fully receiving the results I wanted. Work needed to be done. In meditation I asked, "Where do I start? How do I apply all I learned?" Finally the inspiration came to create a workbook and use it as another tool that would allow me to map out my day using the principles I learned over the past couple of years. A very simple and practical workbook which would help me organize my thoughts and emotions, train and program my mind where and how to focus, and ultimately create my reality. A workbook, short and to the point. So I did just that, I created a workbook and put it to use. I found my days flowed better and started noticing synchronicity all around me. It took the guesswork out of "What should I be doing or thinking now?" I had an understanding of how to utilize my thoughts and emotions so they worked for me instead of against me during the day.

So without hesitation, I share with you your very own personal workbook to help you create your own roadmap and create the life that only you could imagine.

CHAPTER 2

How Do I Use It?

Knowledge and Practice

After spending countless hours reading brilliant pieces of work from past and present day authors, there is one understanding that resonated so clearly with me: life is truly meant to be simple! Its all about knowledge, balance and harmony. To quote Emmet Fox, a new thought spiritual leader, "The expansion of all our problems, the explanation of all our difficulties, and the explanation of our triumphs in life boil down to this: Life is a state of consciousness. That is the beginning and the end. All other steps lead up to that." Expand your consciousness with knowledge and don't be misled to thinking there is only one way to achieve a desired outcome. Unfortunately, we get in our own way with thoughts, ideas and beliefs that most times are not our own. I knew when I created a workbook I needed to keep the "simple" theme in mind allowing life's simplistic nature to shine through. When faced with contrast, especially if it involves disease, I witnessed how quickly going down a complex and difficult path could overshadow a simple and natural path to healing because of old belief systems. People tend to seek help from those with the best education from the best schools while ignoring their own *Inner Guidance*. This is because of an old belief running in the background of the subconscious mind that people only must listen to those who have a formal education and a long resume.

I also found that people tend to gravitate towards unique or expensive alternative treatments because of an old belief running in the background that you get what you paid for. Who made those beliefs up? I admit, early on my journey, I did the same thing seeking the best doctors and alternative treatments available. Thankfully, I quickly learned from my teacher during the many retreats I attended that true healing starts from the inside out and the cost is knowledge and understanding, reprogramming your beliefs, breaking down old paradigms, and disciplined meditation. It took time to sift through material but there it was, the simple principle or Ancient Wisdom that echoed throughout generations. The body is designed to heal itself. I am so grateful for the dedication of all the brilliant doctors who helped me along my journey, but what I learned through my experience is I needed to simplify my practices and understanding and go within myself for healing. Knowledge is power and application of that knowledge is key.

So how do you use this workbook? It is designed to present principles in the beginning of the chapter, gain an understanding of that principle, and then take part in an exercise at the end. Explaining core ideas of a particular principle at the beginning of a chapter is necessary for completing an exercise at the end. It is the "understanding" that will set you free of old paradigms or beliefs. You must understand and believe that what you are asking for can be accomplished. The exercises at the end are the tools, the "doing", the work. You see, the simple part is the understanding which is achieved by reading, listening or watching material. Applying the knowledge you gained is the work that must be done throughout the day. **I want to be very clear that in order for you to achieve your desired result you must do work and take action.** Once you form a habit with your thoughts and emotions the work will become second nature. Your job then will be to meditate daily. What are some key principles that play an important role in creating desired outcomes? An understanding in the following:

- **Beliefs** - What is a belief? A belief is something we believe in or accept as truth. We can change beliefs to obtain a desired outcome no matter how long they have been programmed in our subconscious mind. Some of the beliefs that we hold on to is the reason we are held from what we truly desire. Changing the belief or program will help us achieve what we are seeking. In order to achieve the reality you are seeking, you first must believe it can be done. The old saying goes "in order to receive, you must believe". This saying is absolutely true in all that you do.

- **Power of words, thoughts, emotions, intentions and affirmations** - It may sound disarmingly simple, but monitoring your words, thoughts, emotions, feelings and intentions throughout the day can affect you positively or negatively. Using them collectively can provide a powerful tool to help you achieve what you are asking for.

- **Vibration and the Law of Attraction** - Like the Law of Gravity, there is a Law of Attraction that runs in the background of all we do. What does this mean? In short, like attracts like. Understanding that we cannot change this Law and that it impacts all we do will help you to work with it and not against it. Once you mastered this, you can use it as an effective tool for creating.

- **Meditation** - Guided and non-guided meditations are both powerful tools to help quiet your mind and break down resistance. By doing these simple acts you will allow your inner guidance to do what it was intended to do.

- **Feeling Based Prayer** - There is a 5th mode of prayer which is also referred to as the "feeling based prayer." It is a different way to pray using the principles of the Law of Attraction. This practice could be the most effective tool in your tool box of deliberate creation.

- **The Physical Body** - Treating our body like a temple is important as well. Sending yourself loving thoughts and feeding it with good food and exercise will help you find inner balance and harmony.

Understanding these basic principles offered me clarity. They opened my mind to a different way of thinking and allowed me the ability to see beyond traditional treatment options. Participating in the exercises in the following chapters will put these principles to use. The completed exercises will become key tools that can be used to help deliberately create a reality. For me, they helped me create optimal well being in my body. They also helped me find inner balance and harmony. But before we can do anything we must believe. The very first step of achieving anything in life involves believing we can. The understanding in the power of one's belief was demonstrated in the works of Jesus thousands of years ago when he would ask the question to everyone he helped, "Do you believe you can be healed?" The power of ones belief is also found in the present day through the work of Dr. Bruce Lipton. He teaches how the power of ones belief system can alter our genetic expression. Our belief systems are powerful and can hold us from all that we are asking. As I emphasized earlier, there is work to be done so let's get to work and open our minds to all the possibilities this beautiful life has to offer. Let's shift ourself to an optimal state of being by creating a gratitude list. All the works I read talk about the importance of gratitude so lets start with a simple exercise that will shift us into a state of Joy.

OLD OUR HAND

Gratitude helps ignite powerful emotions and feelings within our heart center. Igniting these feelings will bring us similar feelings like it and shift us into a better state of being. Being thankful for what you already have is an important way of obtaining what you are asking for. Use this page to write down what you are grateful for. If you are having a hard time finding things to be thankful for, start with powerful statements like, I am thankful for the air I am breathing. I am thankful for the sun rising. I am thankful for the planets being in total balance and harmony with each other. I am thankful for the shelter I have. I am thankful for the fact that I am not chasing after my food. I am thankful for being warm when its cold outside. There is always a way to get yourself into a state of gratitude. Reflect on this list daily and feel free to create as many gratitude lists as you like. There are more pages at the end. Remembering that in order to receive you must feel good. This exercise will provide as a tool to shift you into a state of Joy.

Gratitude List

CHAPTER

3

Conditional Beliefs

Breaking Down Old Paradigms

Attention!! We are not bound to our genes or heredity and we can alter our belief system to anything we want it to be and ultimately obtain any outcome we can see in our mind!! What?!? You mean I am not a victim of my hereditary or genetic coding? While attending one Sedona retreat, my spiritual teacher Anita introduced that concept which left me forever changed. She talked about beliefs and how they affect our physical reality and more. The textbook definition of a belief is 'a set of principles which together form the basis of a religion, philosophy or moral code.' She told a story of a group of men in their 70's who were part of a 1980's experiment conducted by a Harvard psychologist named Dr. Ellen Langer. The subjects were in good health but aging left its mark. Dr. Langer wanted to test the belief that aging could be a mind-set. She asked the men to spend 5 days at a converted monastery. Before they left, the subjects were assessed with dexterity, grip strength, flexibility, hearing and vision, memory and cognition. When they passed through the door, they entered into a time warp filled with 1950's artifacts. They spoke about the 50's in present tense. Nothing — no mirrors, no modern-day clothing, no photos except portraits of their much younger selves — spoiled the illusion that they had shaken off 22 years. At the end of their stay, the men were tested again. On several measures, they outperformed a control group that came earlier to the monastery but didn't imagine themselves back into the skin of their younger selves. They were encouraged to only reminisce. The first group that acted "as if" were suppler, showed greater manual dexterity and sat taller — just as Langer had guessed. They were changing their belief that your health deteriorates with age. Perhaps most improbable, their sight improved. The experimental subjects told Langer they had "put their mind in an earlier time," and their bodies went along for the ride. This added value to Langer's experiment that the mind can alter your physical reality. I could not believe that I was just hearing of this. That's all I could think of. Imagine if we could teach this principle in schools?

After hearing this story, my mind opened to even more possibilities. The word belief kept popping into my consciousness. This experiment provided proof that merely "saying" positive words is not enough to cause desired physical change. It certainly may enhance a mood but actually the physical changes would require a bit more focus. Altering ones feelings and acting "as if", whether true or not, can have a positive effect in ones physical reality. It also is a key component for creative manifestation. If this experiment worked for the men after 5 days, what would it do for me if I lived my life believing and acting as if I was cured? And again, how come studies like this aren't flooding the mainstream media?

This was fascinating! I had so many questions for my spiritual teacher and she had so many testimonies to what I was beginning to believe. Our lives are truly a product of our thoughts, feelings, emotions and most important, beliefs. I wanted to know more and continued traveling to Sedona learning more concepts that were new to me, but very old in origin. On one Sedona retreat in 2016, Anita showed a clip of Dr. Bruce Lipton, a stem cell biologist who taught medical students for 20 years at the University of Wisconsin. Dr. Lipton's resume goes on but what he is most known for is his book *The Biology of Belief, Unleashing the Power of Consciousness, Matter and Miracles*. His book teaches that your beliefs control your physical reality. His book forever changed me. He presented stunning new scientific discoveries about the biochemical effects of the brain's functioning to show that all the cells of your body are affected by your thoughts. He demonstrates how the new science of **epigenetics** is revolutionizing our understanding of the link between mind and matter, and the profound effects it has on our personal lives and the collective life of our species.

After educating myself with Dr. Lipton's work, any leftover doubt I had questioning modern day medicine and the decisions I was making became clear. I now had the proof from a medical perspective and could confidently communicate with my amazing doctors about my health. Dr. Bruce Lipton connected the missing link for me between science and spirituality. He provided the scientific framework for the mind/body/spirit connection and is laying the foundation for a consciousness-based understanding of biology. He explained epigenetics, a new field in the study of genes, and how our environment and emotions create our genetic expression. This was such an amazing discovery because basically he proved that there is no genetic determinism or hereditary other than the genetic blueprint you are born with, eye color, hair color etc. Epigenetics teaches how our environment and belief system alters our genetic expression. Dr. Lipton wrote of his proven experiments in his book. One study was even published at Stanford University over 20 years ago. Dr. Lipton's work provided me the reason "why" I needed to heal from within.

His experiments also offered the explanation why the 70 year old men had such positive results after 5 days. They were starting to believe by acting on every level in their bodies that they were in their earlier years. This is fascinating to me because I just read that a famous celebrity had a mastectomy based off of her belief of the genetic possibility of getting breast cancer. I immediately thought what?!? Why didn't she know about Dr. Lipton and his research?

One of the testimonies Dr. Lipton shared was from the religious radical group in North Carolina that believed that their God will always protect them from danger. Their belief of that statement was so strong that it allowed them the ability to drink small amounts of cyanide and be bit by poisonous snakes with hardly any negative results. They were unaffected! That's right, they lived. Even though this Baptist group can survive these harsh poisons Dr. Lipton suggested we should not try drinking cyanid because that belief system is theirs and not ours. Their belief as a collective whole is why they have little or no effects of the poison. Again to be clear, each of us has our own set of beliefs. Just because one group believes in something doesn't mean it is the same for us. We need to reprogram. In another testimony from an interview, Dr. Lipton spoke of a tribe that believes their health gets better with age. This tribe believes as a collective group that they get youthful looking, and physically faster and stronger as they age. As a whole that is exactly what happens. I don't know about you, but that's one belief system I would love to adopt. Dr. Lipton's published work along with these two testimonies and Dr. Langer's study provided all the proof I needed to change some old beliefs I had running in the background. We truly are a product of what we think, feel and most important believe.

In the words of Mahatma Gandhi:

"Your beliefs become your thoughts
Your thoughts become your words
Your words become your actions
Your actions become your habits
Your habits become your values
Your values become your destiny"

After learning and digesting all this new found information, what did it mean to me? That ultimately whatever is happening on a genetic level has no effect on me or my children's outcomes. What we believe to be is! But how do I change my belief system? It became clear the more I asked that question that I needed to develop a set of tools to reprogram my subconscious. This brought me much ease and comfort. How many people do you know that will say, "Well I am going to get cancer or other illnesses because my parents did?" or "It's in my genes." I hear it all the time so learning these principles offered me freedom. I researched further to see how I could start applying what I was learning into my experience. How can I rewrite a program that would offer optimal health and abundance?

In the *Biology of Belief* Dr. Lipton teaches that the subconscious mind controls 90% of our body's activities and functions. It stores data so we don't have to repeat the task of learning over and over such as walking, riding a bike, speaking, learning the alphabet etc. We download most of what we need the first 7 years of our life. Sometimes we can download programs that may not suit us and we are not even aware that they are controlling our lives on a conscious level because they are stored in our subconscious. To keep these concepts **extremely** simple, let's use Dr. Lipton's analogy of our subconscious being like the hard drive of a computer. If we wanted to rewrite data on our computer's hard drive, you couldn't just talk to the computer screen and expect your computer to rewrite what you are asking, you would have to type using a keyboard and press save. There is action needed. Our brain is similar to that in nature. We have to take action to rewrite unwanted programming. And the beautiful part of this is that it doesn't matter how long the programs are running 30 years or 3 seconds, they can be deleted and replaced in the same manner. Our brain doesn't recognize concepts of time.

There are different ways to changing our programming. The main idea is to tap into the subconscious in a way or language it understands. There is one process that Dr. Lipton references called PSYCH-K developed by Rob Williams. Rob has a Bachelor of Arts Degree in Philosophy from the University of California, at Los Angeles, and a Masters Degree in Counseling and Personnel Services from the University of Colorado. He is President of The Myrddin Corporation, and Director of the PSYCH-K Centre International. PSYCH-K is a simple and direct way to change self-limiting beliefs at the subconscious level of the mind, where nearly all human behavior originates, both constructive and destructive. Its overall goal is to accelerate individual and global spiritual evolution by aligning subconscious beliefs with conscious wisdom from the world's great spiritual and intellectual traditions. I did not explore the PSYCH-K process until after I healed my body, but I did research Rob's work and found it to be an effective option in changing ones beliefs. I encourage you to explore his work. Other reprogramming methods that Dr. Lipton suggested were hypnosis and affirmations. For the sake of simplicity, I decided to use affirmations and explored several teachers.

One teacher that resonated with me was the beautiful Louise Hay, an American motivational author and the founder of Hay House. She authored several New Thought self-help books, including the 1984 book, *You Can Heal Your Life*. Faced with much contrast throughout her life, Louise explained that she created her reality by eliminating old negative thoughts/ words from her vocabulary and focused only on positive affirmations which provided her positive transformation. The idea of words, feelings and emotions having an actual effect on my daily life was a new concept for me. Deep inside I knew that keeping a positive mindset along with using positive words felt good but never knew I could use them along with adding feelings to create a tool to reprogram my subconscious. As I stated earlier, merely saying an affirmation or thinking positive thoughts certainly helps shift your consciousness into a state of joy, but if you want to rewrite a program, you need to find a way to speak in a language that your subconscious understands. At the same time I was learning about the power of affirmations, I was also learning the power in the simple act of dropping our awareness or focus to our heart center. Focusing attention to our hearts, slowing down our breath and feeling the affirmations creates a hot line or pathway to our subconscious mind.

This process of reprogramming resonated with me. I tried to be mindful as much as I could to negative words and negative thought patterns and did not stress if they arose. I just refocused my mind to something or someone I knew made me happy. When reprogramming, I would state an affirmation while adding the feeling of what it would feel like when my affirmation became a reality. After a few short weeks of **feeling** the affirmations throughout the day, the behavioral change was obvious. My life became more peaceful, joyous and harmonious than ever before. I was shaping my reality into what I wanted it to be. I was experiencing synchronistic events and knew if contrast presented, I could refocus by adjusting my thoughts.

I recommend reading these concepts multiple times because the more you begin to become aware, the more information you will be able to process. As I said earlier, it was like listening to another language when someone said to me that I was the creator of my own reality and I can change old belief systems. But now, I understand fully and could not imagine my life any way but the one I create it to be.

Before we begin the affirmation exercises, I thought it might be a good idea to talk further about the importance of heart-brain harmonizing. This coherence understanding will ensure we know how to connect our heart and brain, a key component that ensures the reprogramming is taking place.

CHAPTER
4

Heart-Brain Harmonizing

A way to tap into our subconscious

In the previous chapter, we learned about the power of our belief system and how our beliefs affect our physical reality. We learned from Dr. Lipton that we can change our conditioned beliefs by reprogramming our subconscious mind in a couple of different ways. I chose to use affirmations. As I stated, we cannot just merely say an affirmation or think positively to change or reprogram our subconscious, but we must speak in a language familiar to it. Focusing our attention or awareness to our hearts, slowing down our breath and concentrating on one or all of the following four feelings will create a pathway into our subconscious mind. Focusing on the feelings of *care, appreciation, gratitude* and *compassion* will ignite this heart harmonizing effect. Some of us need clarity when thinking about the difference between gratitude and appreciation. Here is a simple comparison:

Gratitude is when we are grateful for something or someone which allows us to be thankful.

Appreciation is when a person is able to notice the good in someone. This allows us to see the good in people and actions during our interactions.

This heart-brain connection, or harmonizing effect, provides a hotline into our subconscious. Affirmation work should be introduced right after the connection is made. It is when the reprogramming takes place. Lets explore another source of information that has provided much research on the importance of harmonizing the heart and brain; the Institute of Heart Math.

In 1991, Doc Childre founded the nonprofit HeartMath Institute. They research and develop reliable, scientifically based tools that bridge the connection between heart and mind. This empowers people to greatly reduce stress, increase resilience and unlock their natural intuitive guidance for making better choices. Most of us have been taught in school that the heart is constantly responding to "orders" sent by the brain in the form of neural signals. However, it is not as commonly known that *the heart actually sends more signals to the brain than the brain sends to the heart!* Moreover, these heart signals have a significant effect on brain function—influencing emotional processing as well as higher cognitive faculties such as attention, perception, memory, and problem-solving. In other words, not only does the heart respond to the brain, but the brain continuously responds to the heart.

The effect of heart activity on brain function has been researched extensively over the past 40 years. Earlier research mainly examined the effects of heart activity occurring on a very short time scale—over several consecutive heartbeats at maximum. Scientists at the HeartMath Institute have extended this body of scientific research by looking at how *larger-scale patterns* of heart activity affect the brain's functioning. HeartMath research has demonstrated that different patterns of heart activity (which accompany different emotional states) have distinct effects on cognitive and emotional function. During stress and negative emotions, when the heart rhythm pattern is erratic and disordered, the corresponding pattern of neural signals traveling from the heart to the brain *inhibits* higher cognitive functions. This limits our ability to think clearly, remember, learn, reason, and make effective decisions. (This helps explain why we may often act impulsively and unwisely when we're under stress.) The heart's input to the brain during stressful or negative emotions also has a profound effect on the brain's emotional processes—actually serving to reinforce the emotional experience of stress.

In contrast, the more ordered and stable pattern of the heart's input to the brain during positive emotional states has the opposite effect—it *facilitates* cognitive function and reinforces positive feelings and emotional stability. This means that learning to generate increased heart rhythm coherence, by sustaining positive emotions, not only benefits the entire body, but also profoundly affects how we perceive, think, feel, and perform.

Below is an exercise called the Institute of Heart Math Quick Coherence Technique and should be used in accompaniment with affirmation work to provide the language or pathways needed for reprogramming. I know I stated this several times but it is never enough. In order to reprogram or produce change, we must add feeling to our affirmations or prayer work. The exercise below helps us focus our attention to the feelings of our heart so we can rewrite unwanted programs in our subconscious.

The Institute of Heart Math - Quick Coherence Technique

The quick coherence technique will help you find a feeling of ease and inner harmony that will be reflected in your heart rhythms. The heart is a primary generator of rhythm in your body, influencing brain processes that control your nervous system, cognitive function and emotion. More coherent heart rhythms facilitate brain function, allowing you more access to your higher intelligence so you can improve your focus, creativity, intuition, and higher level decision making. When you're in heart rhythm coherence you perform at your best, or what athletes call being in the zone. You feel confident, positive, focused and calm yet energized. There are three steps.

STEP 1 - Heart Focus

Focus your attention on the area around your heart, the area in the center of your chest. If you prefer, the first couple of times you try, place your hand over the center of your chest to help keep your attention in the heart area.

STEP 2 - Heart Breathing

Breath deeply but normally and feel as if your breath is coming in and going out through your heart area. As you inhale, feel as if your breath is flowing in through the heart, and as you exhale, feel it leaving through this area. Breath slowly and casually, a little deeper than you normally would. Continue breathing with ease until you find a natural inner rhythm that feels good to you.

STEP 3 - Heart Feeling

As you maintain your heart focus and heart breathing, activate a positive feeling. Recall a time when you felt good inside, and try to re-experience the feeling. One of the easiest ways to generate a positive heart-based feeling is to remember a special place you've been to or the love you feel for a close friend or family member or a treasured pet. **This is the most important step**. Usually seeing/ imagining baby animals or human babies will make you smile.

WHEN TO USE THIS EXERCISE

When you're starting to feel drained, physically or emotionally, especially if you feel emotions that are causing frustration, irritation, anxiety or stress. Using Quick Coherence at the onset of less intense negative emotions can keep them from escalating into something worse. This technique is especially useful after you've had an emotional blow-up to bring yourself back into balance quickly. You can do this anytime, anywhere and no one will know you're doing it. In less than one minute, it creates positive changes in your heart rhythms, sending powerful signals to the brain that can improve how you're feeling. Apply this one minute technique first thing in the morning, before or during phone calls or meetings, in the middle of a difficult conversation, when you are feeling overwhelmed or pressed for time, or anytime you simply want to practice increasing your coherence. Especially use this when using affirmations when you are creating a particular reality. It also helps with coordination, speed and fluidity in your actions.

Chapter

5

The Power of Placebos/Nocebos

It's A Matter of Believing

Another fascinating testimony illustrating the power of our minds and belief systems is recognized through Dr. Lipton's experiments using what doctors call *placebo* effects. The placebo effect is recognized in traditional medical approaches and scientific experiments. Dr. Lipton chose the term the *belief effect* to stress that our perceptions, whether they are accurate or inaccurate, equally impact our behavior and our bodies. I like that term better because it is more truthful in its meaning. Unfortunately, the placebo effect is quickly glossed over in medical books so that students can focus on treating a patient with drugs and surgery. Dr. Lipton, who taught medical students for 20 years, says that is a big mistake. He goes on to say that the placebo effect should be a major topic in medical school because it shows the power of our internal resources. The power of our mind should not be dismissed when doctors are learning about treatment. When I read this in his book, I felt so empowered. A famous line immediately entered my mind from one of my favorite movies The Wizard of Oz, "You had the power all along, my dear."

I found one experiment Dr. Lipton wrote about especially proved the power of our minds. A Baylor School of Medicine study, published in 2002 in the New England Journal of Medicine, evaluated surgery for patients with severe, debilitating knee pain. (Mosley, et al 2002) The lead of the study, Dr. Bruce Mosley, "knew" that knee surgery helped his patients: "All good surgeons know there is no placebo effect in surgery." But Moseley was trying to figure out which part of the surgery was giving his patients relief. The patients in the study were divided into three groups. Moseley shaved the damaged cartilage in the knee of one group. For another group, he flushed out the knee joint, removing material thought to be causing the inflammatory effect. Both of these constitute standard treatment for arthritic knees. The third group got "fake" surgery. The patient was sedated. Moseley made three standard incisions and then talked and acted just as he would have during a real surgery-he even splashed salt water to simulate the sound of the knee-washing procedure. After forty minutes, Moseley sewed up the incisions as if he had done the surgery. All three groups were prescribed the same postoperative care, which included an exercise program.

The results were shocking. Yes, the groups who received surgery, as expected, improved. But the placebo group improved just as much as the other two groups! The results were clear to Moseley: "My skills as a surgeon had no benefit on these patients. The entire benefit of surgery for osteoarthritis of the knee was the placebo effect." Television news programs graphically illustrated the stunning results. Footage showed members of the placebo group walking and playing basketball doing things they could not do before their "surgery". The placebo patients didn't find out for two years that they had gotten fake surgery. One member of the placebo group Tim Perez, who walked with a cane before his surgery, is now able to play basketball with his grandchildren. He told the Discovery Channel "In this world anything is possible when you put your mind to it. I know that your mind can work miracles." Studies have shown the placebo effect to be powerful in treating other diseases, including asthma, Parkinson's and depression to name a few. Dr. Lipton's book offers more cases and goes into detail if you want more information. I recommend reading as many cases as possible to seed your consciousness into believing that healing is a matter of mind.

Although many in the medical profession are aware of the placebo effect, few have considered its implications for self-healing. If positive thinking and believing can pull you out of depression and ignite inner healing, consider what negative thinking can do. When that same mind is engaged in negative suggestions that can damage health, the negative effects are referred to as the *nocebo* effect.

Dr. Lipton explains that in medicine, the nocebo effect can be as powerful as the placebo effect. The nocebo effect is something you want to keep in mind when you visit a doctor's office. Sometimes, their words and their demeanor can convey hope-deflating messages to their patients. This can work against you even for the most subtle diagnosis. In one chapter, Dr. Lipton cited the Discovery Health Channel's 2003 program "Placebo: Mind Over Medicine". One of the most notable segments featured a Nashville physician, Clifton Meadow, who has been reflecting on the potential power of the nocebo effect for thirty years. In 1974 Meadow had a patient, Sam Londe, a retired shoe salesman suffering from cancer of the esophagus, a condition that was at the time considered 100 percent fatal. Londe was treated for that cancer, but everyone in the medical community "knew" that his esophageal cancer would recur. So it was no surprise when Londe died a few weeks after his diagnosis.

The surprise came after Londe's death when an autopsy found very little cancer in his body, certainly not enough to kill him. There were a couple of spots in the liver and one in the lung, but there was not a trace of esophageal cancer that everyone thought had killed him. Mr.

Londe died not from cancer but the *belief* that the cancer was going to kill him. It was't only Mr. Londe's belief, but everyone around him who believed it as well. We are all connected as we will read about in upcoming chapters. These experiments and studies that Dr. Lipton writes about in his book offered me a new way of thinking about the beliefs I hold in my subconscious and also the beliefs the world that surrounds me hold. I mentioned this earlier, that we can adapt negative beliefs that are not our own. Thankfully, to great minds such as Dr. Lipton, we can reprogram those beliefs that aren't serving us well into beliefs that can shape our reality to what we are wanting. I know that is the reason I am able to remain in a healing state. I believe that there is another way to dealing with my disease other than the traditional methods available. No matter what any one else says, including my doctors, I know I will live a long and harmonious life. I know my physical, emotional, spiritual well being is a matter of what I believe. I will always have the utmost respect for the medical communities especially to all who have tried to help me, however, I know from my personal experience there is much, much more than treating a physical body.

So far, we learned about the principle of beliefs and their power. We also learned that one way we can reprogram our subconscious is by using affirmations. In order for the affirmations to truly work for reprogramming purposes, we must create a pathway into our subconscious mind. An effective way to do this is by igniting feelings within our heart center which we learned earlier.

Below you will find Louise Hay's positive affirmations and language reprogramming exercises. Remembering your mind is like a computer, when you go back into old behavioral thought patterns, choose one statement and **think, say and feel the affirmation as much as you can.** See and feel it done already until it becomes a habit and ultimately a belief. It may sound simple, but affirmations are an extremely effective tool that helped me reprogram my subconscious to work for me and I continue to use them daily. There is room to create your own affirmations. Please keep in mind, that the idea is to use them; this is part of the work I mention often. In order for change, you must take action. These affirmations are to be used as a tool to create a feeling of gratitude that you already received what you are asking to experience.

Language Reprogramming/Re-Creating

Lack/Abundance - Remove all negative words, thoughts, and intentions. Practice making all actions and reactions come from a point of love, non-judgement, and positiveness. Refocus on abundance; diminish focus on lack. Even if you are experiencing lack, replace the feeling of lack with the feeling of abundance.

Create what you want for yourself through acting as if it is yours already. You must identify with, feel, believe and become that which you desire. Allow it to become so much a part of your consciousness that you truly feel as if you have it in your life already. Your manifestation comes into physical form through the understanding that what you desire already is yours to have. By acknowledging have, you will demonstrate have. A consciousness of need, produces more need.

Saying these affirmations are effective but attaching an emotion makes them that much more powerful. Pick an area that resonates with you. Pick one positive thought pattern and say and feel one or all statements. Remember how the placebo experiments demonstrated how powerful our minds truly are. Begin by thinking, saying and and, most important, feeling the joy the statement brings you. Say them as much as you can remember throughout the day. This takes practice but the more you do the work, the easier and more automatic this habitual way of thinking comes into effect. Feel free to create your own affirmations.

Desire	Positive Thought Pattern

Language Reprogramming/Re-Creating

Choose one or more of these affirmations in the morning. It's important to choose them before you start your day so you are prepared. Say, think and feel these affirmations throughout the day. Give these intentions time. Do not take notice of your life changing immediately but instead experience the feelings they bring about in your being. Positive change will happen, just be patient and appreciate that what you are asking for is on the way. If the negative thought patterns creep in, adjust accordingly by repeating these positive thought patterns.

Desire	Positive Thought Pattern
Gratitude	• The more gratitude I feel, the more I am aware that the supply is endless. • My day begins and ends with gratitude and Joy. • Abundance flows freely through me. • I awaken today, appreciating everything in sight, and I give thanks.
Happiness	• I now free myself from destructive fears and doubts. • Today is going to be a really good day. • Everything in my life works now and forevermore.
Health	• I am in perfect health. • Wellness is the natural state of my body. • I am pain free and totally in sync with Source. • I am at home in my body. All is well.
Faith	• All is well. Everything is working out for my highest good. Out of this situation only good will come. I am safe. • I am Divinely guided at all times. • I now free myself from destructive fears and doubts.

OLD OUR HAND

Language Reprogramming/Re-Creating

Choose one or more of these affirmations in the morning. It's important to choose them before you start your day so you are prepared. Say, think and feel these affirmations throughout the day. Give these intentions time. Do not take notice of your life changing immediately but instead experience the feelings they bring about in your being. Positive change will happen, just be patient and appreciate that what you are asking for is on the way. If the negative thought patterns creep in, adjust accordingly by repeating these positive thought patterns.

Desire	Positive Thought Pattern
Inspiration	• I go beyond barriers to possibilities. • This is a new day. I begin anew and claim and create all that is good. And so it is. • I accept my power.
Love	• I rejoice in the love I encounter every day. • I am loved; I let love in I am kind to myself. I live in peace and gratitude. • I am worth loving and there is love all around me. • My heart is open. I allow my love to flow freely. I love myself. I Love others and others love me.
Self-Love	• All that I seek is already within me. • I deserve the best, and I accept it now. All my needs and desires are met before I even ask. • I choose to feel good about myself each day. Every morning I remind myself that I can make the choice to feel good. This is a new habit to cultivate.
Success	• I radiate success and prosperity wherever I turn. • Everything I touch is a success. • I am open and receptive to new avenues of income.
Acceptance	• I deeply and completely love and accept myself. • I love myself just the way I am. • I am at home in my body. All is well.
Forgiveness	• I now choose to release all hurt and resentment. • I forgive everyone in my past for all perceived wrongs. I release them with love. • I forgive myself and set myself free.

OLD OUR HAND

Exercise: (Re)Creating

List what you do not like about yourself, what you feel is wrong in your life and what you want to change (life, circumstances, lack, relationship, job, peace. etc).

Now list what you want for yourself and what you want to be or have.

Next, re-create negatives into positives using I AM or I have affirmations. Reiterate a list of I AM and I have desires until you believe that you already have that desire and that you are that desire. When your subconscious is fully reprogrammed, you will see changes. Remember to ignite the feelings that those statements bring you.

Things I Do Not Have	Things I Have
I will have/need money.	I Have abundance; I Am abundant.
I will find a loving partner.	I Have a loving partner; I Love myself.

CHAPTER

6

The Law of Attraction

It's All About Vibration

Growing up I always had an understanding that whatever feelings or intentions you put out into the Universe comes back to you. I imagine I heard that phrase a bunch of times from my mom or elders who taught us to be nice to others if we wanted the same treatment in return. I taught the same understanding to my children and would remind them often to treat others as they wanted to be treated. I never really knew how literal that statement was or that it could alter our physical reality. Our ancestors and many others before taught us what I know now are the keys to manifestation. I was introduced to Esther, Jerry and Abraham Hicks who taught me about the Law of Attraction. Understanding the principles of this law and how they work helped shape my physical reality.

During one of my retreats to Sedona, Anita showed a DVD of a woman named Esther Hicks. Esther is an inspirational speaker and author who presented numerous workshops along with her husband Jerry. Esther would go into a state of consciousness that allowed Abraham, a group consciousness, to speak through her. Abraham, in simple terms, is a beautiful piece of the Divine who offers lessons to us "humans" as they so eloquently refer to us. I was extremely confused but mesmerized by the Truth Abraham spoke. In each lecture I listened to, Abraham used unfamiliar terms like the *Law of Attraction*, *Vibration*, *Vortex*, the *Art of Allowing* and *Vibrational Reality*. I was very confused by it all. What was this Law of Attraction that Esther was speaking of? The Truth that Esther/Abraham spoke about in these segments, along with the sarcasm and humor captivated me during the day and brought me a great tool to use and share with my family. They made the Law of Attraction easy to understand and I hope to share with you my interpretation and explain how that knowledge helped me return my body to a state of healing. Many people admire Esther and Abraham's work such as Wayne Dyer, Oprah, Louise Hay and many others. I want to shout out a huge thank you to Esther/Jerry Hicks and Abraham for they helped me through some of my darkest hours. I could go on forever talking about Esther/Abraham but as promised I will keep this workbook short and to the point. I recommend watching, reading and listening to any material by Esther, Jerry and the teachings of Abraham for they have helped transform my life into what it is today.

During that same retreat Anita handed out two sheets. One was titled the *Basic Principle of Life* written by Emmet Fox, a New Thought spiritual leader of the early 20th century, famous for his large Divine Science church services held in New York City during the Great Depression. The paragraph that resonated so well with me was:

"Your so called physical body is the embodiment of a part of your consciousness. The kind of work you are doing - whether you are in work that you love, or whether you are doing drudgery that you hate is the expression of your consciousness at that point. The kind of people that you attract into your life, are the expression of your consciousness about your fellow men. And of course, the entire principle can be condensed into three words: Like Attracts Like."

The other handout was by Ernest Holmes' *The Law of Mind* from a book he wrote called *This Thing Called You*. He was an American New Thought writer, teacher, and leader and was the founder of a Spiritual movement known as Religious Science, a part of the greater New Thought movement, whose spiritual philosophy is known as "The Science of Mind." He was the author of *The Science of Mind* and numerous other metaphysical books, and the founder of *Science of Mind* magazine. To no surprise, he spoke of the same principles:

"When you think with complete conviction, the Law of Mind will operate on your thought exactly as you think it, for the thing, condition or person you are thinking about. The principle you are using has been scientifically demonstrated. It is now merely a question of how effectively you believe it."

I was now learning from Anita the same concept that I heard early in my journey by my brother's friends when they said that I was attracting my disease into my life and that we create our own reality. What amazes me the most is that Ernest Holmes and Emmet Fox transitioned in the mid 1900's and taught the same message that this beautiful woman Esther Hicks teaches today in the year 2018. I left Arizona with a wealth of knowledge and passion, thanks to Anita, and knew to obtain well-being I needed to apply all that I learned about Beliefs, Vibration and the Law of Attraction.

One of the words commonly used by anyone teaching the Law of Attraction is Vibration. That word, like belief, became a part of my thoughts all day everyday. What is vibration and what does it mean to me and my health and creating a reality? After some research, I understood it to be that we are vibratory beings vibrating at different frequencies. Much like a guitar needing tuning when its out of tune, when our bodies are in dis-cord, or dis-ease, they need tuning to restore the cells to the frequency of well-being. I know that this sounds simple, but as I started to research I learned that most holistic modalities that are used to treat our bodies are simple and make perfect common sense in their approach. I learned that the vibration within our bodies can be measured. If we are out of tune vibrationally we can tune our bodies back to balance using vibrational tools to achieve vibrational healing. I found that vibrational healing traced back to the beginning of time and is used in eastern medicine regularly. I equated what I learned about vibration to how my feelings could change from bad to good just by hearing and feeling a good song. Before I started going to Sedona and started my chemotherapy treatments, I would have Friday night dance parties, playing music and dancing. I must say that participating in dance parties limited my side effects and brought my mood up when I felt deflated. I know that music, which is vibration, was helping me restore my body to its original state of healing. Someone once said to me that celebrations serve as a great tool for healing. I celebrated every Friday night which helped me feel good during challenging times. I started wondering, can sound healing really be a legitimate way to help restore a physical body when in discord?

As I continued to educate myself on vibrational healing and its effects on the body, I found vibrational healing music on YouTube and began listening to frequency healing music. I listened throughout the day and night in hopes to restore my cells to the frequency of well being. Jonathan Goldman, an international authority on sound healing and a pioneer in the field of harmonics, became my resource. His work always left me feeing uplifted. Learning about the power of one's beliefs through Dr. Lipton was life changing, but it wasn't until I found Dr. Mitchell Gaynor, a board-certified medical oncologist, internist, and hematologist, that I felt total ease with the decisions I was making. Dr. Gaynor treated cancer traditionally for most of his career and was a best-selling author of numerous books, including *Nurture Nature Nurture Health: Your Health* and *The Environment; The Healing Power of Sound: Recovery from Life-Threatening Illness Using Sound*. Also, Dr. Gaynor is the founder and president of Gaynor Integrative Oncology in Manhattan, he had been a clinical assistant professor at Weill Cornell Medical College, also in Manhattan, and director of medical oncology at the school's Center for Integrative Medicine. Like Dr. Lipton, Dr. Gaynor subscribed to the belief that what happens to us on the emotional and spiritual level affects us physiologically. It wasn't until he had an experience with a Tibetan monk who taught him about the power of vibrational healing that he started to add alternative medicine into his practice with amazing results. I bought his book *The Healing Power of Sound* and watched his lecture on YouTube titled *The Harmonic Destiny of Healing*. I was captivated as Dr. Gaynor explained that our genes are altered by the environment, not by genetic determinism which was exactly what Dr. Lipton explained in his book. I was also intrigued how he used sound healing as a form of treatment. Epigentics was explained to me by both doctors in such a way that made perfect sense. Two brilliant minds teaching groundbreaking information that changes everything we currently know in the field of genetics. They are both brilliant doctors ahead of their time and such a gift to humanity.

Dr. Gaynor and Dr. Lipton's studies helped me with the decision to implement vibrational sound healing into my tool box. Using external tools to tune my body, such as tuning forks, crystal bowls, and other sound modalities was a wonderful way to manipulate my vibration in a physical manner. My body responded so well that I wanted to learn more about vibration and find ways to tune my body daily. I found Deborah Van Dyke, author, sound healer and musician when searching for healing frequency music on iTunes. Deborah explained on one of her cd's that we live in a sea of sound that is a current of vibration that keeps the whole universe in motion. All of life is vibration. Every atom is constantly moving. Sound is the force that organizes all matter and it effects each atom in our body. Deborah taught me that ancient people have always known the profound effect that sound has on the body, mind and Spirit. When we use certain tools such as tuning forks, or crystal singing bowls, their vibrational tones stimulate the restoration of harmony within us. Their tones resonate strongly with the liquid crystalline substances in our bodies and cause rhythmic balance in our cells. I felt balance and harmony when using these tools.

This fascinated me. Every cell and organ function at different frequencies and are constantly moving within our bodies. I pictured all my cells, organs, tissues and glands working together to create a unique me. Operating at their own frequencies to create our own unique Inner Symphony. Our inner symphony is also able to communicate with other frequencies. Not only within our bodies, but all there is. I remember Anita used many sound tools during her treatments and my body felt amazing and balanced afterward. I knew including sound therapies is a must when it comes to healing a body but how can we use sound along with vibration and the Law of Attraction to create our realities? To answer that question fully I still needed clarity about vibration and the Law of Attraction so I continued to develop a deeper understanding of these principles. I couldn't help but think constantly why am I just learning about this now? I asked Anita who explained that many years ago, the great minds of the past gave us the keys or directions on how to use the Law of Attraction to create. If you read the original work of Jesus Christ and Buddha, they spoke of the Law of Attraction in their own words:

Jesus

"As a man thinks, so is he." – Proverbs 23:7 King James Version (KJV)

"We do not look at the things which are seen, but the things which are not seen. For the things which are seen are temporary, but the things which are not seen are eternal."
- 2 Corinthians 4:18 New International Version (NIV)

"Truly I tell you," Jesus replied, "if you have faith and do not doubt, not only will you do what was done to the fig tree, but even if you say to this mountain, 'Be lifted up and thrown into the sea,' it will happen. If you believe, you will receive." - Matthew 21:22 (NIV)

Buddha

"The mind is everything. What you think you become."

"All that we are is the result of what we have thought."

"To enjoy good health, to bring true happiness to one's family to bring peace to all, one must first discipline and control one's own mind. If a man can control his mind he can find the way to Enlightenment, and all wisdom and virtue will naturally come to him."

"We are shaped by our thoughts; we become what we think. When the mind is pure, joy follows like a shadow that never leaves."

These amazing teachers and ancestors knew that vibrations affect our current realities and also left clues on how to use the Law of Attraction to change our realities if we wanted. Our beliefs, the Law of Attraction and vibration principles have been around for lifetimes and are still being taught today by beautiful minds. Still searching for clarity on how to use what I was learning to create a reality, I knew I needed to tap into my own internal guidance. I needed to truly understand these principles and come up with a set of tools that I could use as part of a daily practice. I needed to form a new positive thought pattern. I searched further for answers and explored vibration and frequency further. I learned that everything that exists holds a certain frequency. In the words of Nikola Tesla, a Serbian-American inventor, electrical engineer, mechanical engineer, physicist, and futurist who is best known for his contributions to the design of the modern alternating current (AC) electricity supply system:

"If you want to find the secrets of the universe, think in terms of energy, frequency and vibration."

And as Einstein, a German-born theoretical physicist who developed the theory of relativity put it best:

"Everything is energy and that's all there is to it. Match the frequency of the reality you want and you cannot help but get that reality. It can be no other way. This is not philosophy. This is physics."

In scientific terms, these powerhouses spoke of the effects of vibration and frequency and how they can effect a physical reality. Just match the frequency, Like Attracts Like the message seems to be the same from great minds of all eras. Things were starting to become clear to me. I read these quotes before but never understood their meaning until now. They too were giving us directions to create our realities.

Anita introduced Dr. Masaru Emoto, a Japanese author, researcher, photographer and entrepreneur, who said that human consciousness has an effect on the molecular structure of water. She showed us a DVD where Dr. Emoto explained that because our bodies are made up of mostly water, we can alter our physical reality if we change our thoughts, intentions, words and emotions. Wow!! I must say this realization, opened my mind to endless possibilities. On previous retreats, I learned about the power of our beliefs and how our mind can affect our physical bodies. I also learned about vibration and frequency and how sound can effect our bodies, but what I did not really understand is the power of our thoughts and intentions until I saw Dr. Emoto's experiments. I did not know that our thoughts, intentions and words can affect our physical bodies and be measured. The concept that we create our realities was becoming more and more clear. I watched as Dr. Emoto performed multiple experiments, one involving rice, and was so fascinated by its results that I decided to use his rice experiment for my daughter's 8th grade science project.

According to his experiment, we needed to put rice into mason jars half way and fill it with water enough to cover the rice. We were to say hateful words to one of the jars, loving words to another jar, and ignore the 3rd jar. We did this for 30 days and found amazing results. The rice in the jar that we spoke loving words to remained unaffected, the jar we spoke hateful words to started to rot and the rice in the other jar started to get moldy but not as much as the hate jar. How does this happen? You see Tesla, Einstein, Dr. Emoto, Abraham, and other great teachers taught us that everything created carries a vibration and frequency, including words, intentions, thoughts and emotions. Words of love carry a high beautiful frequency and vibration and words of hate carry a very low vibration and frequency. My family and friends were able to understand on a tangible level after they saw the effects of Dr. Emoto's simple yet powerful rice experiment that my daughter used for a science project.

Dr. Emoto's power of words, thoughts, intentions and emotions can be seen in this YouTube clip https://www.youtube.com/watch?v=au4qx_I8KEU or by visiting his website at http://www.masaru-emoto.net/english/water-crystal.html. Here you will **see** a beautiful demonstration of the power of your thoughts, intentions, words and emotions. Seeing these experiments validated even more the possibility that we can create our realities. The higher vibrational words thoughts and feelings we hold onto, the higher vibration we experience within our own bodies and life experiences. And because our bodies are made up of mostly water and respond to vibration, then we can expect that the higher vibration it holds, the healthier we are.

Another great and fascinating teacher is Dr. David Hawkins, MD., Phd. He is a widely known authority within the fields of consciousness research and spirituality. He has written and taught from the unique perspective of an experienced clinician, scientist, and mystic. He has a measure of frequency of such states of consciousness and words. Through testing, he was able to provide a map of consciousness. The higher the frequencies, the more peaceful state of consciousness and the happier the soul. In one of Dr. Hawkins books I read he gave an example of how powerful the mind is in relation to its beliefs. He told a story of one of his patients who had two personalities. When the patient was in one personality, let's call him Tony, the patient believed he was overweight and would hold onto calories and gain physical weight, however, when he was his other personality, let's call him Nick, he believed he was thin and that he can eat and drink whatever he wanted and would start to look thin. The same patient Nick would drop the weight by just *"believing and feeling"* he was thin.

Dr. Hawkins stated the results were immediately noticeable when the patient would change personalities. With the knowledge and proof that words, thoughts and feelings carry a vibration, we can understand how his physical reality followed his thought pattern and produced a physical change. The most important thing we must not forget is that change would not have been possible without the underlying *belief* that it could. Dr. Hawkin's patients believed he could change and demonstrated this with different personalities.

I found Dr. Hawkins testimony fascinating because again it validated the power of human beliefs, vibration, emotions, feelings, thoughts and words and how they work together. I now had the answer to my earlier questions. Can we change our physical reality by first believing we can, and then working with the Law of Attraction and vibration? The answer is yes we can by using our beliefs, thoughts, emotions and feelings as tools. How comforting is it to know we have a tool no matter where we go. Our Minds! All we need is the awareness and a road map and we can utilize our minds as a powerful and effective tool to create any reality we choose. Along with our internal guidance, it's truly all we need. I have many more testimonies proving these teachings, including many of my own, but I want to keep this book simple.

Now that we have a general understanding of the Law of Attraction, and the power of words and vibration, lets follow some simple and extremely effective exercises to utilize the knowledge we learned thus far and start creating realities we want. First lets take a closer look at the brilliant Dr. Hawkins' measure of emotions and how they register on the vibrational scale and effect our consciousness. In simple terms, the better we are feeling the higher the vibration and the more good we attract into our lives.

Measuring Vibration

Developing an understanding that our thoughts, feelings and emotions can be measured helped me to understand how our emotions can affect us on an energetic level. You can see by the chart below when we are feeling anger, grief, or shame we can expect our energy levels to be low; however, when we are experiencing, peace, love and joy than we can expect higher energy levels. Based on what we previously learned, you must feel good to receive. You can clearly see how being mindful of how you feel can act as a tool to creating your reality just by changing the way you think. It's a simple decision, just state I choose Joy in this moment. That simple statement can shift your being into a more positive place.

Emotions	Energy Levels
Enlightenment	700-1000
Peace	600
Joy	540
Love	500
Reason	400
Acceptance	350
Willingness	310
Neutrality	250
Courage	200
Pride	175
Anger	150
Desire	125
Fear	100
Grief	75
Apathy	50
Guilt	30
Shame	20

The Creative Process

Steps to Deliberately Create your Reality

With all this new and life-changing knowledge I learned, I realized just "knowing" the information was not enough. The knowledge was obviously an important part in creating, but just reading, understanding and listening to the teaching was not enough. I needed to utilize all I learned and put the information together to create a plan or workflow. There must be action on our parts to create a change. My feeling was validated after listening to many lectures and reading much material, that in order for us to create, there must be a process we follow. Although, this process is explained by many brilliant minds, I found the Teachings of Abraham to be the simplest to understand.

When I first really understood the concept that my thoughts, feelings, words and emotions can impact my physical reality, I would drive myself crazy trying to monitor every thought as it would enter in and out of my mind. It seemed daunting because we process thousands of thoughts a day. While listening to one of Abraham's segments, they offered a simple and effective explanation on how to monitor our thoughts and words. Abraham said we are born with an *Internal Guidance System* known as our emotions and feelings. It is almost impossible to monitor all our thoughts but easy to monitor how we feel. And further, we cannot receive anything we are asking, unless our vibration is high and we are "feeling" good. I wanted to create a feeling of optimal well-being and became mindful to how I felt in each moment. I tried to adjust to a better feeling if I wasn't feeling great. Monitoring my feelings seemed like an easy enough first step to creating but could this be that simple? Based on what I was learning the answer was a very loud yes.

Abraham explained that there is a Source, God, Divine, Universe, Divine Essence, I AM presence, or however you want to refer to this beautiful energy, functioning at this very moment working for us. The Source energy is wanting to give us all that we are asking for. But this beautiful Divine Essence operates using a high vibration and only can align to what we are asking through a vibrational match. What that means in familiar language is that Source is communicating through a feeling good station, and unless we match the feeling good frequency that Source is on without static or resistance, we cannot receive what we are asking for. I could not help but connect the two principles I just learned about the Law of Attraction and Vibration. Everything was beginning to make sense.

Abraham states that the Universe is like a catalogue and there are Laws it must follow to deliver what we are asking. You could see the Law of Gravity in full effect when you jump in the air. You know without any resistance or doubt that you will come back down and not drift away. The Law of Gravity cannot be turned off or ignored. The Law of Attraction follows the same rules and is constantly running in the background. It states that like thoughts, feelings and emotions attract other thoughts, feelings and emotions that match their frequency. Like attracts like. The Law of Attraction also states that we can only receive what we are asking for if we raise our vibration to match a frequency to that of which we are asking. The Law of Attraction does just as it states: it attracts thoughts, emotions and feelings that are similar in vibration. So if you are feeling, thinking, intending negative thoughts, you can bet the Law of Attraction will do its job and deliver and match what you are projecting. Neither The Law of Gravity nor the Law of Attraction will disappoint us with their results. What you ask for must be given, we just have to match the frequency, as Einstein states, and that reality will be yours.

Abraham also taught us that we have a buffer. There is a 17 second rule that gives us time to change our thoughts or intentions before other thoughts like it "stick". It can work either way for us. If you continue a thought for more than 17 seconds, it builds momentum by attracting another thought like it. The one thought can attract more thoughts like it and start to shape our realities by building momentum. We can experience this when we wake up in a bad mood. If you do not make any efforts to change your state, the next thing you know you might stub your toe on the bed, and as your frustration grows and momentum builds further, you might find yourself caught in traffic. You get the point. Thoughts attract thoughts like it. You can stop this momentum by changing your state. Try doing whatever you can to feel good. Music helps me. Anything that helps you to shift your thinking to good feeling thoughts is fine. There aren't any rules but to just feel good. Think of the most joyous or happiest time in your life, a favorite trip you took, baby animals, or anything that would bring a smile to your face. Try anything that will redirect your thoughts to a happier time. You are the creator so you must take action to create.

Negative thoughts are also known as resistance. Negative thoughts such as doubt, fear, anger, etc. are all considered resistance and are the only thing holding us from receiving what we are asking for. Sometimes when negative thoughts build momentum, they could become difficult to stop. A quick way to shut down negative momentum is to shift your thought pattern. As we said earlier, you can change your negative thought to a positive one by thinking of something that you know brings you joy. It sounds simple and it's supposed to. Shifting your thought's attention from something sad to something happy, if practiced for a few weeks, will form a habit. It becomes more automatic. Like braces help redirect your teeth to perfection, you can shape your reality by redirecting your thought pattern. The more you choose happiness in the moment and redirect your thoughts to ones that serve you, the easier it becomes. You will start to attract more harmony into your life. This is how you form a habit or change a belief.

Another way to shut down resistance is meditation. You can shed resistance by sitting quietly, focusing your attention to your heart and watching your breath for 10-15 minutes a day. This simple tool is so powerful and can be used anytime and anywhere. If I could not sit quietly at home, I would take a break at work and sit in the bathroom stall. As I said, it can be practiced anywhere, it's your attention to your heart center and breath that matters. If redirecting your thoughts or meditation does not help stop the resistance, you can take a nap. Sleep is a time when all resistance or negative thoughts cease. Shifting your thoughts, meditation and sleep are effective ways to stop negative thoughts which will ultimately slow down momentum. But what if we want to create a reality?

Using the same Law of Attraction and vibration principles, you can deliberately create a reality by building positive momentum. The first thing to do is to find time to focus on a positive or good feeling thought and emotion for more than 17 seconds. Holding the positive thought for 17 seconds will allow another thought of its kind to attach to it and build momentum. And if you add emotion to it, the momentum becomes much more powerful. I know this sounds to simple to be true, but I can attest to its validity through my own experiences. I understood it by imagining different stations on a radio. You can't receive the frequency 106.7fm if your radio is set to 106.7am. Just won't happen. Exactly like that, we cannot receive all that we are asking unless we adjust our vibration to that of Source or the Divine which is at a higher vibration or frequency. I will now offer in the simplest terms how I interpreted the creative process to work and how I use it to manifest, or create my reality. I taught this to my "children", 23, 22, 21 and 15, and they too attest to its ease and effectiveness and use it often.

Here are the steps explained by Abraham that I followed to manifest experiences into my life. There are five of them.

- **Step 1 - *Ask.*** Ask for and it is Given says Abraham, and ironically, they are the same words that Jesus spoke almost two thousand years ago, "Ask and it Shall Be Given." Life and its contrast causes you to launch these vibrational rockets of desire all day everyday. Contrast is the knowing of what you do not want, whether it is lack of money, lack of health, lack of success, or whatever the contrast is, and then knowing what you do want, abundance, well being, success, etc. There isn't anything too big to

Ask the Universe for. Look around you. You can witness the beauty that the Universe creates and orchestrates so effortlessly so ask away. As Abraham states, if you think it is a big task, then it is. The Universe is like a catalogue so put your order of desire in for the reality you want to create.

- **Step 2 - *Source answers*.** As soon as you launch your rocket of desire, it is fulfilled by Source. That is the Law. The Vortex gathers your desire and a vibrational reality is assembled waiting for you to be a cooperative component of what you asked for. If a desire is created in one's mind, there is an immediate fulfillment created by Source every time no matter what.

- **Step 3 - *Allow*.** You have to find a way to become a vibrational match to your desire before it can manifest. What that means is that you have to feel the emotion of your manifestation as if it happened already. Remembering what Dr. Lipton taught about beliefs, you must feel good and believe that you can receive what you are asking. It is important to limit any resistance or doubt. Doubt from yourself or others, which is why I highly recommend keeping your creative process to yourself so you can eliminate the doubt of others. Meditation is the best way to release resistance. When you quiet your mind, you get out of your own way. Meditation is an essential everyday tool, which I will describe later, and must be utilized in the creative process. Like seeds in the soil, we know if taken care of properly with water and sunlight, will blossom into beautiful flowers. Our "Asking" is like a seed we plant, and the nurturing is the feeling good and knowing it will be done. We must know our manifestation is on its way, while limiting doubt, and remember not to keep looking to see if it's "here". Just know it is done much like a mother does when she knows a baby is on the way.

- **Step 4 - *Mastering Step 3*.** Become more in tune to your surroundings and what makes you feel good. You have arrived to the place where you are totally mindful of how you feel and know how to utilize your *internal guidance system* which is your indication. There is NO wobble. You know how to feel good so you can receive and totally care about how you feel. You must know what you are asking for is on its way much like you know that when you jump, you will come down. No matter what, every time.

- **Step 5 - *Contrast comes go back to Step 1*.** Contrast presents for more deliberate creating. Don't get thrown off when contrast and negative emotions come again but accept it, and be able to think forward eagerly because you see it as an opportunity to grow more fully. Truly understand the power and the value of returning to step 1 over and over. Negative emotion is just guidance which just leads us to more deliberate creation. To sum up the Law of Attraction and how it works is that the Universe is vibration. We are vibratory beings who communicate to the Universe through a vibrational reality. Everything we asked for is given, but we must match or tune in to the frequency of what we are asking. We are constantly asking for change and then having to match a frequency to receive it. Because the Universe doesn't differentiate thought and understands a vibration, if we are thinking "lack" the vibrational match of "lack" is what we receive. We must act "as if" what we are asking for is here even when we cannot see it in present moment.

It's the allowing, knowing and our unwavering Faith that will shed the resistance so we can match the frequency or vibration of the desired creative reality. Our Source, God, Divine reside in a very high vibration and will not come down to our low vibration when we are not feeling good. The key is to only partake in things that make you feel good most of your day and avoid negativity you may find in people, tv shows, and surroundings as much as you can. I can attest to the fact when I started to mind my own vibration, everything else that used to bother me didn't anymore. The more I made a conscious effort to be happy and love myself, the more things that used to bother me took care of themselves. Abraham mentioned several times, if one person in a household raised their vibration, then the entire house would benefit. I made a true effort to surround myself with joy as much as I could and attracted more and more harmonious joyful experiences because of it. I know first hand how hard it is to not fall into what I call the "rabbit hole" when contrast comes. You feel like you are being hit with a 2 x 4. I had many reasons to want to give up and probably would have if I did not find these amazing teachers who taught that we can shape our realities into anything we want them to be. No matter what illusion is being presented in your experience. Once I truly understood the principles and applied them, my body reacted and matched the vibrational frequency of well being. I have many miraculous moments that I want to share and will another time, but what's most important is to stay focused. *Know* that there is no physical state, no matter how bad it is, that cannot return to its original form of unconditional love and well being. Something else Abraham taught me that resonated so well and I use often is that, everything you see in your now reality is past tense, old news and that all that is to be created is in your Vortex of possibility. It's in your hands depending on what vibrational disc you choose to be on. Vibrational discs are the feelings that you choose to feel in the moment: sad, angry, happy, joyous etc. After all, we have choices to feel any way we want to. It truly is just that, a choice. If you choose happiness in this moment and hold that feeling, thought and intention long enough, it will find others like it and before you know it you are creating your reality. It is also known as our free will.

Below is an exercise that applies all five steps of the Creative Process. It is a simple, yet powerful exercise. I learned of it listening to one of Abraham's segments and applied it to my own experience. My results were amazing. I shared it with family and friends and they too had similar results. The key is to be disciplined and not give in to doubt and fear if they present themselves. Live in the "now" and learn to relish each moment and love your self. Self love is the key to one's happiness.

HOLD OUR HAND

The Law of Attraction - The 3o day Creative Process

ASK

1. This Creative Process is supposed to be very simple. The first step is to look at things you would like to attract into your life and ask to experience them. Use this list to write down the things you are asking for and only read them on the first day. When you are done "placing your order", put the list away and **know** that it's on its way.

2. On a separate piece of paper, write a thank you letter to the Universe addressing all the things on your ask list. Write the letter in past tense as if you already manifested what you asked for. Be sure to include emotion and really feel the Joy as if your asks were fulfilled already. It's very important to include emotions as read your letter. Next, try to hold an image in your mind of what it would look like if your manifestations already happened. Read, **feel** and see your thank you letter twice a day for 30 days. I read my letter before work and before bed. There is no wrong or right time of day to read your list, just do it with meaning. Once you read your letter, your job is to just feel good the rest of the day. The whole key to this process is to make sure you are in a good feeling place.

3. Create another list of things that bring you Joy. These things should be as simple as hugging your dog or dancing, not things that you need to make great efforts to achieve or rely on. Make an effort everyday to do at least one thing on the list. If you cannot find something that makes you happy, think of the simple things such as I am happy for the air I have to breath, the roof over my head to keep me warm, or the fact I don't have to hunt down food to eat.

4. Feel good as much as you can everyday knowing whatever you are asking for is on the way. Be diligent and mindful. Don't look to see if what you are asking is here, just let it manifest and know it's on the way. Also, meditate at least once a day for 10 minutes to release any resistance you might be holding.

HOLD OUR HAND

Focus daily on these things that bring you joy. Whether you focus on one thing as much as you can or focus on all of them makes no difference for it is in the joy and feeling good that will bring about change. Take time to sit and appreciate the joy that these things bring you.

Things That Bring Me Joy

HOLD OUR HAND

Here is a sample of what this exercise looks like. It's just a sample and please feel free to listen to your own inner guidance so you may ask what you heart truly desires.

ASK
I would like to have a healthy body.
I would like to experience clean beautiful skin.
I would like to have healthy relationships in school and at home.
I would like to have a better relationship with my spouse, mom or dad.
I would like more clarity and focus in sports or in the workplace.
I would like to live abundantly.

OLD OUR HAND

Sample Thank You Letter

Dear Universe,

I want to say thank you for all the amazing manifestations that are a part of my life now. My body feels so healthy as it moves about the day. I am so thankful that the Divine Pattern within is functioning in harmony without any blockages or interruptions. Thank you for this well being I am feeling. I have unlimited energy going about my day and am able to feel rejuvenated. My skin looks flawless and is getting more supple with age. Thank you for this beautiful, flawless, smooth and soft skin. It glows with perfection. I want to thank you for the wonderful relationships I have at school and in the workplace. It feels so good and comforting to go about my day with these harmonious people who surround me. I feel a sense of ease and peace with the relationships that I encounter everyday. I feel the love I have inside for myself and I AM attracting more love into my life because of that. Thank you.

I am so thankful for the amazing clarity and focus I can tap into. I am so grateful for the vision I have on the field, court, and in the workplace. I know that if contrast comes, I can readjust my thoughts to work for me by thinking of something that makes me happy immediately. No matter how bad it seems in the moment. I know thanks to you there is never a situation I can't come back from by refocusing. I know I can utilize the law of attraction to work for me by changing my thoughts and feelings. Thank you for helping me see so clearly.

I am super excited and appreciative about the financial freedom I now have. I love the way I live with ease and freedom experiencing this beautiful life that I am co creating with you. I thank you for teaching me about the abundance that lies within. I was able to pay off all debt and live with total freedom. Thank you for all you taught me and continue to teach me daily. I am so Blessed to share this journey with you.

Much Love And Appreciation,
Ann

This is a sample letter that I wrote to answer all that I asked for in the Ask exercise. Write your own letter for all you asked for. Write your letter using sentences as if all you asked for is present already as I did above. Read the letter you write with passion, going through each sentence expressing your sincerest gratitude and acting as if it is manifested or created already. Let the feeling of completion come from your heart and not your head. It is best to read this after doing the heart harmonizing meditation I mentioned earlier. When you experience the heart harmonizing technique, you complete a pathway into your subconscious which is a good time for you to introduce this thank you letter.

CHAPTER
8

The Science of Miracles

The Quantum Language of Healing, Peace, Feeling and Belief

On another retreat, Anita showed us a documentary called the Science of Miracles narrated by Gregg Braden. Gregg Braden is a five-time New York Times best-selling author, and is internationally renowned as a pioneer in bridging science, spirituality and human potential! From 1979 to 1990 Gregg worked for Fortune 500 companies such as Cisco Systems, Philips Petroleum and Martin Marietta Aerospace as a problem solver during times of crisis. He continues problem-solving today as he weaves modern science and the wisdom preserved in remote monasteries and forgotten texts into real world solutions. He has also argued that human emotions affect DNA and that collective prayer may have healing physical effects.

In the DVD, we watched as Gregg spoke of an experiment that took place in the late 1800's. There were talks about the findings of an energy field that existed around our body known as the etheric field. The Michelson-Morley experiment was conducted to determine if this etheric field did in fact exist and if it connects each of us like the scientists suggested. Unfortunately, based off that experiment, scientists claimed that everything appeared to be separate in nature holding no validity of an etheric field or any other energy body that connected us. So from the late 1880s until the early 1990's science was based off the belief that what happened in one area does not effect another.

Between 1993 and the year 2000 a series of experiments were conducted by accredited and academic institutions. These experiments are shaking the field of science. Why is this important? These new experiments proved that the scientists in the 1800's were correct in their theory that we are all connected. Gregg explained that ancient text and modern day scientists now both agree that we are connected to each other and everything in the Universe through a subtle field of energy. This field of energy is described by western scientists as a net or a web that creates an underlying fabric of all creation. The recent scientific findings support the belief of the energy field around us and that we are all connected to the same energetic web. It also supports that our connection to this web has a direct impact on everything that is connected to it as well. This field of energy we are learning, has been here since the very beginning and is an intelligent field that responds deeply to human emotion. What does this mean? This validates all that we learned in the previous chapters and the reason why we are able to create our reality with our thoughts, feelings and emotions. There are many amazing "Truths" to this documentary the Science of Miracles, but for our purposes, we will just focus on the 5th Mode of Prayer also know as the *feeling based prayer*.

Knowing of this energetic tapestry that we are all connected to will help us understand the 5th mode of prayer, also known as the *feeling based prayer*. This prayer teaches us that we must '"feel" the feeling and act "as if" the prayer has already been answered. It is in that feeling process that we speak to the forces of creation, allowing the world to respond to us through the energetic web that we are all connected to. So praying while feeling powerless, angry, desperate, etc. and asking for something to be done is actually working against us. It attracts negative emotions, such as, desperation and despair, that are present in the prayer. We are continuously asking, igniting the feelings of something needs to be done. But when we participate in the 5th Mode of Prayer, it is the **"feeling"** of **"knowing"** that what we are asking has already been answered. In that moment, we actually empower the energy field to mirror back to us those changes to whatever it is we are asking. Learning about the feeling based prayer's principles, I could not ignore how they mirrored the principles of the Law of Attraction; like attracts like. The principles delivered the same directions for creating, act *as if* your prayer is answered and attract like thoughts, emotions and feelings to create the reality you are desiring.

Gregg, early in the 1990s, had an opportunity to experience this feeling based prayer. At that time the Desert South West was experiencing one of the worst droughts in history. A Native American friend of Gregg invited him to a place in the high deserts in Northern New Mexico to share in a prayer *of* rain. Gregg agreed and off they went. They met at a stone circle. His friend removed his shoes and stepped into the circle in his bare feet and thanked all of his ancestors. He then honored the four directions and turned his back to Gregg and held his hands in a prayer position for just a few seconds. He then turned to Gregg and said he was hungry. Gregg was puzzled asking him why he didn't share in the prayer *for* rain. He looked at Gregg and said because if we prayed *for* rain, then rain could never happen. His friend explained that the moment you prayer *for* something to occur you just acknowledged that it does not exist in that moment. When Gregg's friend prayed, he felt the feeling of what it would feel like to have rain in his Pueblo village. He said he smelled what the rain falling off the earth and walls would smell like. He felt the feeling of what the rain feels like on his naked feet in the mud, and in that way of prayer, he opened the door to possibility. Later that afternoon, Gregg was watching the weather maps and the drought that happened for so long suddenly changed and that night they experienced rain.

It wasn't until I saw another segment in the Science of Miracles that I truly without a doubt believed in all I was learning. It was a piece Gregg introduced from the Medicineless Hospital in Beijing. This piece highlighted one of its patients who had inoperable bladder cancer. They showed a woman laying on a table receiving an ultrasound. We were able to see a still sonogram picture of her tumor on one side of the screen and on the other side of the sonogram screen, we were able to watch live as the tumor disappeared. This tumor that western medical doctors agreed could not be treated. She went to this Medicineless Hospital in Beijing *believing* they could treat her. We got to witness this amazing healing in this documentary. The three practitioners were standing over this woman and administering the feeling base prayer. They felt in their heart center what it would feel like to see this woman's cancer disappear. They also acknowledged that it would be gone now. They were all in agreement with the emotions that this treatment would bring and the time she would be healed which was immediately. Her belief and willingness to accept the treatment from the three practitioners were a big part of her healing. The healing would not have taken place without her belief that she could be treated. While the sonogram technician kept a live picture, we were able to watch the tumor disappear. The practitioners were trained to connect in a way that Gregg's Native American friend did and through their belief system along with the patient, we watched the tumor disappear. I was dumbfounded. So many of my friends are no longer with me and I have been put through very aggressive and painful treatments. The knowledge I gained through Anita and other sources made me wonder why I didn't hear of this type of treatment in this country?

This was amazing and I am in awe every time I watch the procedure. You can also watch this by going to youtube and typing in the search bar *Healing Cancer in 3 Minutes with the Mind*. This knowledge again validated everything I was learning about the Law of Attraction and deliberately creating. It also validated that before any healing can take place we must first believe in what we are doing, just as we talked about in the placebo effect chapter. The patients believed they were receiving the surgery, so their bodies healed. Or how the 75 year old men were able to reverse the aging process by believing they were in another time. Everything I was learning was beginning to fit together nicely like a puzzle does, piece by piece.

I started using the feeling based prayer exercise below daily. The 30 day creative process exercise we explored earlier is also a feeling based prayer. On the many retreats I learned so much, but so much of the same knowledge. So many ways of teaching the basic principles that Jesus and Buddha taught in their work. We must *speak from the heart*, in a language that the Divine understands using our emotions and *act as if* what we were asking for already existed. It was magnificent. All of what I speak of is the same message passed down from many generations. It's just a matter of what you believe in, speaking from your heart, using emotions, and acting as if your prayers are answered already no matter what's presented in front of you. When you start to read quotes, you can see these principles are what great minds used to create their masterpieces.

"When you believe in a thing, believe in it all the way, implicitly and unquestionable."
- Walt Disney

"The day science begins to study non-physical phenomena, it will make more progress in one decade than in all the previous centuries of its existence."
- Nikola Tesla

"Imagination is everything. It is the preview of life's coming attractions."
- Albert Einstein

"A man is but the product of his thoughts; what he thinks, he becomes."
- Gandhi

"The doctor of the future will give no medicine, but will instruct his patient in the care of the human frame, in diet and in the cause and prevention of disease."
- Thomas Edison

Let's write our own feeling based prayer and use it as another tool to create a desired reality. The more you act as if and believe, the more you will attract what you are asking for into your life experience.

OLD OUR HAND

Keeping Gregg's Native American friend and the Beijing practitioners in mind, let's focus on the 5th mode or feeling based prayer. Sit quietly and think of someone or something you would like to pray for. Now imagine, using as many senses as you can, that your prayer has already been answered. Remember the more you feel and know it has been done, the more powerful your prayer becomes. You must not pay attention to the illusions in front of you. Avoid feelings of fear or doubt. If you are praying for someone, educate them as much as you can so they can understand how important it is to believe in the process. Teach them about the placebos and spontaneous healings that take place. Knowledge is power, the more you learn the more you understand and can believe that we truly can alter our realities. Infuse yourself with positive material, music, videos etc. Stand firm in your belief that Thy Will Be Done.

Someone or Something I Would Like to Pray for

CHAPTER
9

Meditation: A Powerful Tool

Sit Quietly and Go Within

When I first heard the word meditation I thought that if I wanted to participate I would have to get lost in a remote location and surrender all my worldly possessions. But what I have come to find is it just means to sit quietly, Be Still and Allow. Shut down your mind to the world around you and go within. When we sit quietly, we get rid of resistance which is what holds us back to attracting what we want. Meditation is a required tool when using the Creative Process.

The great Paramhansa Yogananda, an Indian yogi and teacher who introduced millions of Indians and westerners to the teachings of meditation, describes meditation as

"deep concentration on God or one of His aspects." He also described that

"The soul loves to meditate, for in contact with Spirit lies its greatest Joy."

Practiced on a daily basis, it produces astonishing results on all levels of your bodies: physical, mental, emotional, and spiritual. It connects you with your own inner powers of vitality, clarity, and love. When done deeply, it also gives you an expanded sense of connection with life and an experience of profound joy.

Its physical benefits include:

- Stress reduction.

- Strengthening the immune system.

- Decreased blood pressure and metabolic rates.

- Reduced circulation and detoxification on the blood.

- Reduced signs of aging (in long-time meditators).

- Beneficial changes in the frequency and intensity of brain waves, including an increased frontal lobes of the brain, an area responsible for problem-solving and making positive lifestyle changes.

So how do we meditate? Just sit quietly with yourself. I know for me at first it was almost impossible to quiet my mind. I was the type of person who always had to be busy doing as many activities as I possibly could filling every second of every day. Every piece of literature I found on the Law of Attraction, the Creative Process and tapping into our inner healing potential **required** meditation. Many great teachers taught the same steps. Let's explore the meditation process below. You could record the process using the voice memo app on your phone or just go through the steps in your mind. Makes no difference. Follow the directions below and learn the secret to connecting to the power within.

Quiet Meditation to release resistance:

Sit or lie comfortably.

Close your eyes and begin simply witnessing your breath.

Observe the inflow and outflow of your breath without attempting to control it in anyway. Watch your breath. Just watch it. Just observe it.

You may find that your breathing spontaneously becomes faster or slower, deeper or shallower and even may pause for a time. Allow the changes to occur without resistance or anticipation. Whenever your attention drifts away to a thought in your mind, a sensation in your body, or a sound in your environment, gently return your awareness to your breathing. If you notice thoughts coming in that feel good and that you can't help but receive them, then allow them to come through and pay attention this may be your inner guidance you are tuning to. Continue this breathing meditation for about 5 to 15 minutes.

Your mind is like a muscle; the more you do this, the easier it becomes and the more focus and clarity you gain. Also, this is the time when you release resistance as Abraham teaches us. This is the time you connect to what they call the *vortex* or *inner guidance*. If there is a thought or idea presenting itself that seems almost impossible to let go, pay attention because it may be inspiration coming from within. In time, you will learn how to differentiate between "noisy thoughts" and inspiration from your inner guidance.

I recommend starting with 10 minutes and building up to 15. You can do more if you want but you really only need 10-15 to reset your mind, except for those days where everything seems like it is working against you. Then you can shoot for more and remember if all else fails, you can take a nap. That is a sure way to stop thoughts.

Meditation is my most powerful tool and required for inner peace and creation. Time spent in quiet allows connection to Source where the answers to all creation lie. The above meditation is used to allow guidance to come through. There is another meditation I learned that is similar to the 5th Mode of Prayer or feeling based prayer, and that is *guided meditation*. On the many retreats I attended, Anita walked us through the most beautiful guided meditations. She explained the importance of sitting quietly and connecting to our Source. When we sat and listened to her meditations, I experienced a feeling of love and peace throughout my body that I cannot put into words. She gave us handouts with different meditations to use when we returned home so we could experience the same feelings of peace at home. I used the voice memo app on my iPhone to record my voice. I listen to the recorded meditations as much as I can and am able to go back to the amazing place that she guided us to in Sedona. Here are a few meditations that you can use to record your voice, but first lets look at Gregg Braden's powerful *Heart Harmonizing Meditation*. I recommend doing this before any other meditation. It creates a hotline into your subconscious and makes the guided meditations more powerful.

Gregg Braden introduced this *Heart Harmonizing Meditation*. Much like the *Heart Coherence Technique* I mentioned earlier, the *Heart Harmonizing Meditation* is a powerful way to tap into the heart's power. There are approximately 40,000 specialized brain like cells in our heart called sensory neurites. These special cells are concentrated in such a degree that they are actually called the little brain in our heart. They can learn, think and remember independently from the neurons in our brain and they communicate with us separately from the neurons in our brain in a language that we may or may not recognize. We are conditioned to see the world through our brain and if we are lucky at some point in our adult lives we get to connect with our hearts. We have access to these sensory neurites through feelings and meditation. We can work with the brain independently from our heart, which is what most of us do now. And some people can work with the heart independently from our brain. Both of those ways of viewing ourselves are incomplete. When we marry or harmonize the heart and the brain together it creates an extended neural network that makes us different from all other forms of life. This is where our deepest empathy, compassion and intuition comes from. There is something very special about this. When we are able to harmonize the little brain in the heart with the big brain in our head we create so many benefits. We can process information extremely quickly along with 1300 other biochemical reactions. I encourage you to check out Gregg's work on Brain-Heart Harmonizing to see all the benefits. Also, by harmonizing we create a hotline into our subconscious and the best time to introduce affirmations.

Heart Harmonizing Meditation

Bring your awareness to your heart. If you need help focusing, you can lightly touch or cup your heart. Awareness will always follow touch.

Slow down your breathing. Breath through your heart center by inhaling for 5 seconds and exhaling for 5 seconds. When you slow down your breathing, you are telling your body that you feel safe. This will eliminate stress hormones and ignite the healing chemistry in your body. Breath slowly witnessing your breath through your heart center.

Now, keep focusing your attention or awareness to your heart, slowing down your breath. Concentrate on one or all of the following four feelings. Focusing on the feelings of *care*, *appreciation*, *gratitude* and *compassion* will ignite this heart harmonizing effect completing a neural pathway. This will create a pathway into our subconscious mind. Really feel the feelings of each emotion. This meditation should only take a few minutes and should be done with intention and feeling. This is the time to introduce affirmation work or another guided meditation. If you want to listen to this meditation, just type Gregg Braden Heart Harmonizing Meditation in the YouTube search bar. I strongly suggest you listen so that you learn to understand the workflow. You will also learn more about the benefits.

Meditation to bring in the Light

From the Heart of God, I imagine, sense, see, a Divine Golden White Light that comes down through the crown of my head (which I open as I would a book to the center page). This light fills every cell, every tissue, every bone, every organ, every gland, every muscle, every joint, all water and fluids within, all acupuncture points, all meridians, all Nadi and Prana within, with golden white light energy that goes all the way through my body exiting my feet. This beautiful Light passes through the crust of the Earth, the mantle, and anchors firmly into the heart of the earth. I extend this light through my skin and it becomes a column of light that rotates clockwise around me, purifying, electrifying, harmonizing, recalibrating, healing and mending all unwanted negative thoughts, negative beliefs, negative karmic repeating patterns and all negative limiting emotions. So Be It, and So It Is.

Forgiveness Meditation

Keeping your awareness in your heart, let go of all grievances, resentments and regrets. Repeat the following statement right from the Course of Miracles to help you release toxic emotions from your heart:

"Every decision I make is a choice between a grievance and a miracle. I relinquish all regrets, grievances and resentments and choose the miracle." (Say this 3x)

Now think of anyone who you are holding a grudge or a resentment against. Visualize them in your awareness and practice forgiveness recognizing that everyone is doing their best from their state of consciousness. Have the intention to forgive others and yourself and any trespasses that might have resulted in pain. Having let go of resentments, grievances and regrets and having embraced forgiveness, bring your attention back to your breath. Touch your face, open your eyes.

Guided Meditation for Health

This is a guided meditation that I used to experience healing. You can record your voice and listen to the voice memo or just visualize the meditation:

Bring your awareness to your heart. Breath in and out of your heart center.
Take a long slow deep breath, hold it for 5 seconds, exhale and repeat: My Mind is Quiet
Take a long slow deep breath, hold it for 5 seconds, exhale and repeat: My Emotions are Calm
Take a long slow deep breath, hold it for 5 seconds, exhale and repeat: My Body is Relaxed

Start by witnessing your breath. Witness the inflow and outflow of your breath through your heart center. Visualize your body in a moment of time when you were at your best physically. Hold images in your mind of events you wanted to see happen, picturing yourself in total health both inside and out. Imagine what it feels like to be pain free or how your body felt when you were in perfect heath. Walk your mind through segments of a day, living and feeling the life you desire and imagine that it already happened trying to truly experience all the 5 senses. The moment you start the meditation feel the feelings of appreciation in your heart center, knowing that your prayer is answered. Think of something you would like to see happen. I would do this feeling based prayer before bedtime and when I woke in the morning.

CHAPTER
10

My Body, My Temple

Nourish Your Body with High Frequency Foods

Keeping my body well nourished with food and exercise was an important part of healing as well. Many different sources agree that we should treat our body as if it is a Temple. Before my trips to Sedona, I worked with a nutritionist who helped me get my body back into remission for a few months with just nutrition. I became a vegan and worked hard keeping my body in a state of healing. I had results and beat cancer with just the nutrition, however the rigor of the regimen took its toll on me. Unfortunately I came out of remission which led me to Sedona. I learned the importance of balance from that experience. After all, how many times did we hear our grandmothers say, "Everything in moderation." It's been a long journey, but I now know that maintaining a **manageable** nutritional and physical program is important, but even more important, is maintaining balance and moderation. It is the balance and moderation that will ensure continued success. So if we adapt a basic nutrition regimen coupled with some type of exercise, like walking, dancing, yoga etc. we will ensure that we are tending to our temples. There are a few other easy, short modalities and processes that I adapted into a daily regimen.

In January 2016, I met a Dr. Bill Akpinar, D.D.S, D.M.D, Dr. Ac., Ph.D, who taught me about the importance of QiGong (pronounced Chee Kung). In his book, **Shaolin Yoga QiGong**, he describes this ancient Chinese practice so perfectly as "movement meditation". He wrote about the process and explains how to go through these exercises and refers to them as the Eight Pieces of Brocade, a depiction handed down to him in a Shaolin Temple. He also explained how physically beneficial it is, on a cellular level, and actually showed pictures of a cell before and after. You clearly can see the disfigured cell rebalance to its healthy state just from his slides. Why I loved his interpretation of QiGong is because he kept it simple. I adapted the 8 movements of Brocade, which takes about 10 minutes, into my daily regimen. You can find his book and even order a DVD online.

If anyone wants to explore this practice further, here is a YouTube link showing how to do the **Eight Pieces of Brocade, with Master Zhong XueChao**, https://www.youtube.com/watch?v=445Fz8AQvX8. His website http://www.wudangdao.com.

A friend of mine gave me a copy of a book titled, **The Little Book of Energy Medicine**, by Donna Eden. Donna is a veteran teacher of energy medicine. This book immediately resonated with everything else I was already using in my daily regimen. It offered a simple approach to clearing the physical energy bodies around us. Donna, explains that based off of Einstein's formula E-mc^2 which states that **"energy is all there is"**, There is flowing energy around and in us that needs balancing. I adapted her quick 5 minute technique into my regimen. Her simple techniques include:

- Tapping, massaging or holding specific energy points on the skin.

- Tracing or swirling your hands above your skin along specific energy pathways.

- Practicing exercises or postures designed to bring a feeling of calm and renewal.

- Surrounding an area with healing energies.

Her book is beautifully written and nice to have for reference and reminding. She also offers her morning routine in a YouTube piece. Here is Donna Eden's website incase you want to learn more about Energy Medicine. http://LearnEnergyMedicine.com.

Donna Eden's Daily Energy Routine [OFFICIAL VERSION]https://www.youtube.com/watch?v=Di5Ua44iuXc

Alkalinity and pH Levels

One important common approach everyone in alternative medicine focuses on is monitoring the alkalinity of the body. I first heard about the importance of a body's pH level and the impact it has on the physical body from Richard, my brother's scientist friend. He explained that our body is like a swimming pool and in order to function properly it should maintain a pH level of 7.2. A pH less than 7.2 causes the body to become acidic allowing it to become a breeding ground for bacteria and viruses. He also explained keeping the body at a high pH level, or too alkaline, can cause imbalances as well. A pH of 7.2 is ideal. It's the pH level we are born with and ironically the pH of the ocean. Food can impact the alkalinity in our bodies. Below is a chart of foods and their pH levels.

pH Level	Foods
10.0	raw spinach, raw broccoli, artichokes, raw celery, cauliflower, carrots, potato skins, alfafla grass, red cabbage collards, seaweed, onions, asparagus, brussel spouts, cucumbers, lemons, lime, watermelon
9.0	olive oil, herbal & green tea, most lettuce, raw zucchini, sweet potato, raw peas, sprouted grains, raw eggplant, alfalfa sprouts, raw green beans, beets & greens, blueberries, pears, mangoes, papayas, figs & dates, tangerines, melons, kiwi, grapes
8.0	apples, almonds, avocados, tomatoes, fresh corn, mushrooms, turnips, olives, soybeans, bell peppers, radishes, rhubarb, pineapple, cherries, wild rice, strawberries, apricots, cantaloupe, honeydew, peaches
7.0	butter (fresh, unsalted), cream (fresh, raw), milk (raw cow's), margarine, oils, except olive
6.0	coconut, eggs, fish, tea, kidney beans, plums, processed juices, rye bread, brown rice, barley, cocoa, salmon, oats, liver, rice & almond milk
5.0	cooked beans, chicken & turkey, beer, sugar, canned fruit, white rice, potatoes w/o skins, pinto beans, black beans, lentils, butter (salted), rice cakes, cooked corn, wheat bran, rhubarb, molasses, navy beans, garbanzo beans
4.0	coffee, white bread, peanuts, pistachios, beef, blackberries, cranberries, prunes, sweetened fruit juice, wheat, most nuts, tomato sauce, buttermilk, cream cheese, popcorn
3.0	lamb, portk, wine, shellfish, pastries, cheese, soda, black tea, pasta, pickles, chocolate, vinegar, aspartime, processed foods, microwaved foods, stress, worry, lack of sleep, overwork, tobacco smoke

CHAPTER
11

Doesn't Matter What Brought You to Your Knees

Just Matters That You Know You Can Always Rise Up

Whatever it is that brought you to your knees doesn't matter. The pain that got you there is the same whether it's caused by disease, depression, the loss of a job, etc. It doesn't matter the reason, pain is pain and finding a way out of what I call the rabbit hole requires the same principles, starting with self love. Finding time to love yourself and go within is what will bring your body back to balance. The principles in this book will help you gain the knowledge you need to create a new reality; to ignite the power within. Moving past difficulties boils down to an understanding in some basic principles. Knowing what you are wanting, asking for what you want, meditating to receive inner guidance, and most important, falling in love with *you*.

My journey has been full of surprises, difficulties and miraculous occurrences. I often hear people say that they wouldn't survive what I did because they are not as strong willed as me or have as much Faith as I do. I am here to tell you that everyone is equal, and I am not stronger, more faithful or more blessed than anyone else. After everything I learned, the most important thing is that we are One! That is the beginning and the End. You are the creator of your reality. This I know with undeniable faith, and what you do with the knowledge you learn and the action you take will determine how well you *create your masterpiece*.

My beautiful sister in law brought me a sign one day that really touched my heart and I reflect on these words as much as I can remember:

"Let your Faith be stronger than your Fear."

Wherever you are in your journey, I want you to know that Life is only a big deal if you make it one. If you see your dreams in your mind, have Faith and "act as if" in you heart, you will hold your dreams in your hands.

Let Love, and Light and Power Restore the plan on Earth.

Many Blessings now and always.

CHAPTER

12

Resources

Readings, Meditations & Stories to Help Raise Your Vibration

To start the day in the right momentum, I read spiritual/high vibrational material. This passage is included in my daily routine as a reminder of the power of our mind.

The Basic Principle of Life, by Emmet Fox

"The expansion of all of our problems, the explanation of all our difficulties, and the explanation of our triumphs in life boil down to this: Life is a state of consciousness. That is the beginning and the end. All other states but lead up to that."

Some realizations to ponder:

1. It is *my consciousness*, and not the consciousness of others that shapes my life and molds my world.

2. Every single experience in my life, whether 'good' or 'bad,' is created out of the vibration of my consciousness. The higher the vibration, the greater the degree of good in my life.

3. If I continually think about the possibility of being attacked by some form of disease, then I am developing a consciousness of disease, which must out picture itself as a breakdown of the body.

4. I do not work to develop a healthier body. Rather, I work to gain a consciousness of health, a spiritual consciousness of wholeness.

5. If I dwell on limitation and insufficiency in any area of my life, I am building a consciousness of lack, and lack always attracts more lack.

6. If I say 'I can't afford' something, I am building a 'can't afford' consciousness and the laws will bring more things and experiences into my life that I can't afford.

7. In demonstrating an all-sufficiency in my life, I seek the realization that my consciousness of God As My Supply, Is My Supply.

8. If I worry about what others are saying and doing, I am giving my energy to a so-called 'outside power'—which emphasizes the belief in duality and keeps me anchored in the third dimension.

9. I cannot judge the actions of others because they cannot help doing what they are doing. They are simply operating out of their present sense of identity, a particular level of consciousness.

10. If I am uptight, heavy, concerned or anxious about anyone, I am becoming negatively attached to that person, which gives him/her power over me. I cut the cord on anyone who makes me feel less than I am in truth.

I also read the Law of Mind daily.

The Law of Mind, a passage from the book This Thing Called You, by Ernest Holmes

Even God must wait your conscious co-operation before the full light of His presence and the power of His law can be made manifest through you. Your conscious co-operation with Him starts with a realization of the Divine Presence and your union with it. Say:

I know that the Presence and the Power and the Activity of the Living Spirit are in and around me.
I know that the Law of God, which is perfect, is operating through me.
I know that there is One Mind, that Mind is God that Mind is my mind.
There is no fear in this Mind, no memory of fear, no expectation of fear.
This Mind is functioning in me now.

Now make known your desires and accept them as manifested facts in your life.

Every organ, function, action and reaction of your physical being, circulation, assimilation and elimination, are parts of a Divine Pattern which is forever perfect within you. Say:

There is no obstruction to the operation of this pattern.
There is no irritation, agitation, inflammation.
There is no sense of unhappiness or morbidity.
There is no confusion in Spirit.
Therefore, there is no confusion in my Mind.

There is one Divine circulation flowing through me which is never inhibited, retarded or congested.
This circulation is free, complete and perfect, automatically eliminating that which does not belong to pure Spirit.

When you think with complete conviction, the Law of Mind will operate on your thought exactly as you think it, for the thing, condition or person you are thinking about. The repeated experience of thousands during the last fifty years has proved this. The principle you are using has been scientifically demonstrated. Its now merely a question of how effectively you use it. Say:

The Mind within me, being God, is not afraid of anything.
It does not remember any unhappy experience, nor does it anticipate any.
At the center of my being there is complete poise, perfect faith and confidence.
I Am forever one with Spirit, in It and of It.
I Am an individualization of pure Spirit.
There is no condemnation, no judgement, no sense of sin, sinner, mistake, punishment, burden, doubt or fear in me, no bitterness, no hate, no strife.

Reflections from Inspirational Teachers

"Self-love is the knowing that you were created to be completely loved and completely lovable just as you are. When you embrace this truth, the world mirrors that knowing. When you don't feel loved or lovable, it is because you have lost your connection to your spiritual nature. You have lost your connection to your true self.

The path to love clears up a monumental mistake that millions of people make—that someone out there is going to give us something that we don't already have.

This path is never about externals; we become dependent on other people to make us feel totally and permanently loved, yet this expectation will always be defeated because of our inability to develop an unshakable relationship with ourselves.

The great poet Rumi says: *'Everything in the Universe is within you. Ask all from yourself.'*

My hope for you is to fall in love with yourself, your spirit. For when you perceive yourself as Spirit, you will not simply feel love—you will be love. And when you truly find love, you find yourself."
- ***Deepak Chopra***

"When a path opens before us that leads we know not where, don't be afraid to follow it. Our lives are meant to be mysterious journeys, unfolding one step at a time. Often we follow a path worn smooth by the many and in doing so we lose our authenticity, our individuality, our own unique expression. Do not be afraid to lose your way. Out of chaos, clarity will eventually arise. Out of not knowing, something new and unknown will ultimately come. Do not order things too swiftly, wait, and the miracle will appear." - ***Ann Mortifee***

"Anger is one of fear's most potent faces. Before we express our anger to others, the attitude of empowerment is to express your anger as well as your pain to God. He can handle it. The line "Vengeance is mine, safety the Lord" actually means just that. When the anger mounts, call on God. Tell Him first." - ***Marianne Williamson***

"Just as silk worms weave the web of their cocoon and are caught in it, so do humans spin a web of thoughts and beliefs and are then caught in them." - ***Deepak Chopra***

"The mind and the emotions are like wild ponies. They dart this way and that way. It takes patience, love, perseverance and attention to tame a wild creature. You have to understand its ways and work to gain its confidence. You must learn about its fear and seek to heal them. The mind and emotions will serve us faithfully if we offer them our time, attention and understanding. Once tamed, they become mighty allies, willing to carry us powerfully toward our goal." ***Ann Mortifee***

Lastly, there are three true stories about three beautiful people that overcame, what most consider, the impossible. I reflect on them and use them as an inspirational tool to help myself and others.

The first story is about a woman called Anita Moorjani. I read her book called *Dying to Be Me*, in 2 days. She is a testimony to believing in yourself no matter what anyone thinks. She had terminal cancer and came back from a near death experience sharing the most amazing story of survival. I highly recommend you read her book and check her out on YouTube https://www.youtube.com/watch?v=rhcJNJbRJ6U&t=69s and also on her website http://anitamoorjani.com

Another fascinating story is of a man named Morris Goodman who at the age 35 was known as Mr. Success. One of the leading life insurance salesmen in the world, a member of The Million Dollar Round Table and Top Of The Table, Morris had success, fame, fortune, and a brand new airplane. And then things turned upside down. While attempting to land his airplane one afternoon Morris crashed. With his neck broken at C1 and C2, his spinal cord crushed, and every major muscle in his body destroyed, Morris was no longer able to perform any bodily function except to blink his eyes. His injuries were too severe for him to survive.

But the man the doctors dubbed "The Miracle Man" did survive and with a strong faith in God, courage and determination, Morris not only rebuilt his body but also his mind and outlook on life.

Morris feels you too can learn to be happy, have peace of mind, and accomplish all your goals and dreams no matter what hand life deals you.

Today Morris is a highly sought after speaker who travels the world sharing his story with millions of people and teaching his philosophy on goal setting, personal growth and development. You can watch his story on YouTube at https://www.youtube.com/

watch?v=bfKn92klPeU. You can also read his story on his website at http://www.themiracleman.org

The last story is about a man named David Millman. David's story is told in a movie called the Peaceful Warrior. Another beautiful story of the human spirit and learning to love yourself and never giving up. Below is a YouTube clip from the movie that I absolutely love and send to my children as much as I can remember. It is dialogue between David Millman and a mentor known as Socrates. To me, it sums up the importance of living in each and every moment. Here is the YouTube link where I found the dialogue below. https://www.youtube.com/watch?v=31lUwuhE8pc Here is David's website http://www.peacefulwarrior.com

Take out the Trash

Socrates: The Mind is just a reflex organ, it reacts to everything! It fills your head with millions of random thoughts a day. None of those thoughts reveal any more about you than a freckle does at the end of your nose. Take out the Trash. The trash is anything that is keeping you from the only thing that matters. That's the first part of your training. Learning to throw out everything you don't need in here.

Millman: How?

Socrates: This Moment. Here. Now. And when you truly are in the here and now, you will be amazed at what you can do and how well you can do it. When you feel fear, use the sword. Take it up here and cut the mind in ribbons slash through all those regrets and fears and anything else that lives in the past and the future. Life is choice, you can choose to be a victim or anything else you would like to be.

Millman: Just ignore what happened to me?

Socrates: A warrior acts, only a fool reacts. A warrior does not give up what he loves, he finds the love in what he does. A warrior is not about perfection, nor victory or in vulnerability, its about absolute vulnerability. That's the only true courage.

Millman: And what if I can't do it?

Socrates: That's the future, throw it out.

Millman: How do I start?

Socrates: There is no starting or stopping only Doing.

*Socrates: Where are you? **Millman:** Here*

Socrates: What Time is It? *Millman*: Now

Socrates: What are you? *Millman*: This moment.

Sample Daily Spiritual/Mental Guidance

Tools	Goal
Gratitude	I start my day going through all the things I am thankful for. On days that I wake up dark, I make sure to still find something to be grateful for. I am thankful for the air I breath or how the planets balance in perfect harmony or how good the pillow feels under my head. Starting the day with gratitude is important for more feelings like it follow.
Heart Harmonizing Meditation	I listen to Gregg Bradens Heart Harmonizing meditation. You can find his meditation on YouTube. I follow up with my thank you letter or my affirmations.
Thank you letter from the Creative Process Exercise	I read my Thank You letter before I get out of bed and If I can't get to it at that moment, then I read it when I could. It's important never to feel anxious about finding time to read it. It is important to read the letter with feelings of excitement knowing all I asked for is on the way.
Daily Affirmation or Mantra	After the heart harmonizing meditation, I pick some affirmations and reflect on them visualizing and feeling each one. I also reflect on the affirmations throughout the day when I experience "air time". Being prepared and using affirmations throughout the day helps raise and maintain my vibration.
How Do You Feel	Keeping in mind we cannot receive unless we feel good, I am mindful about how I feel throughout the day. I keep my toolbox ready incase contrast comes. Whether it's a song or a thought that brings immediate joy or inspirational material, I am ready incase contrast comes and monitor how I feel as much as I can.
Surround Yourself with Positivity	I avoid negativity. Whether it's people, media, tv shows etc. eliminating as much negative forces when I am deliberately creating a reality is important. I am not suggesting you remove people out of your life permanently, I know sometimes it is impossible, but as you are trying to change something it might be better to redirect your focus for the time being. When they see you starting to change, it may help them ignite an awakening within themselves then you can become their teacher, sharing all that you learned with them. But trust me, let them ask you.
Meditation 10-15 minutes	A necessity and very effective tool. I take some time to be still for at least 10-15 minutes once a day.
Gratitude	Read your Thank you letter or say your list of appreciation so you can fall asleep with positive emotion.
Audio/Video/Literature	As much as I could, I listened, read and watched many great inspirational teachers. I expanded my consciousness to better understand what I was learning. Also, the words themselves, in all the work, carry a high vibration, thus helping me achieve and maintain mine.

Reflections

Reflections

Reflections

Printed in the United States
By Bookmasters